The People's History

Sunderland Bairns

by

Lily Turnbull & Alan Brett

Norma Johnson in the back yard of 47 Dock Street, Monkwearmouth, in 1938.

Three youngsters in Gray Road in 1958. Left to right: Michael Kelly, Gwen Blenkinsop (dressed up like a mother) and Pauline Kelly.

Previous page:
Doreen Tindle (front) at Monkwearmouth Clinic, Dundas Street in 1932.

Copyright © Lily Turnbull & Alan Brett 1998

First published in 1998 by

The People's History
Suite 1
Byron House
Seaham Grange Business Park
Seaham
Co. Durham
SR7 0PW

ISBN 1 902527 21 6

Contents

The Boys' Brigade marching down Dock Street on Good Friday 1959. The girl in the crowd looking on is Gwendaline Deacon.

Sources

Bibliography

Albert Anderson *A Century of Sunderland Cinemas* 1995
Alan Brett *Old Pubs Of Sunderland* 1993
Charlie Buchan *A Lifetime In Football* 1950
Andrew Clark *Pallion and Deptford* 1997
John Yearnshire *Back On The Borough Beat* 1987

Newspapers & Magazines

The Blizzard
Detroit Free Press
The Graphic
The Illustrated London News
Sunderland Echo
Sunderland Herald

School Log Books

The Colliery School
Hasting Hill School
Robinson Street School
St Patrick's School

Reports

Board of Health on Sunderland 1851
East End Commissioners 1896
Employment of Children 1842
Southwick National School 1838
State of the Poor 1797

Introduction

Childhood is a subject that has rarely been covered in books on Sunderland. The 'best years of our lives' – Christmas, Fun and Games and Schooldays are here fondly remembered.

This is not a book just filled with photographs of classes of schoolchildren and sports teams. However, we make no apology for including a number of such pictures. They are a valuable source of social history in themselves.

Nor do we just look at the good times of childhood. While for many local children Wartime was a big adventure, for others it was a case of life and death. The Victoria Hall Disaster is one of the saddest episodes in Sunderland's history. The horrors of child labour in the last century are recalled in Young 'Uns at Work.

As Pat O'Brien points out in her story in Poor Bairns, people 'don't want to remember the hard times: empty bellies, children without shoes on their feet, bad housing, no inside running water and shared outside toilets'.

A class of five-year-olds with their toys at Stansfield Street School in 1925. Sarah Taylor (second from the left in the second row from the front) remembers her mother taking her to school on the first day.

Hylton Castle Juniors, 1960-61 season, John Sampson is second boy from the left, front row.

Acknowledgements

We would like to thank all the individuals and organisations who have helped with this publication.

In particular we appreciate the help of Albert Anderson, Richie Ankers, Joyce Beaton, Billy Bell, Sarah Bell (née Taylor), Jackie Blackburn, Billy Brewster, Graham Brown, Jack Brown, Leslie Brown, Jean Bruce, Ted Campbell, Dave Chester, Harry Clark, Paula Clark, Pauline Clark, St Columba Church, Phil Curtis, Billy Dent, Archie Donaldson, June Dixon (née Martin), Sidney Duncan, Ann Farquhar (née Carr), Peter Gibson, Irene Gibson, Aubrey Harvey, Ann Henderson, Joyce Henderson, Eileen Herbert (née Hedley), Davie Howie, Norma Johnson, Tommy Johnson, Alan Jones, Linda Lawson (née Egan), Gillian Longford, Linda Lowes (née Brown), George Marley, Carol Martin (née Summers), June Martin, Matty Morrison, Pat O'Brien, Geoff Pearson, Norman Pounder, John Price, Joan Quinn, Doreen Robson (née Tindle), Martin Routledge, John Ryan, Elaine Sampson (née Campbell), John Robert Sampson, Annie Scrafton, Father Skelton (St Mary Magdalene Church), Colin Smith, Tommy Smith, Margaret Steabler, Tommy Taylor, George W. Temperley, Liz Turner (née Pearson), Margaret Thynne (née Watts), Jackie Turnbull, Hector M. Tusnan, Billy Wood, Ian Wright, Mrs Wrightson, John Yearnshire.

Northeast Press

Phil Hall, Ashley Sutherland and staff at Sunderland City Library.

Sunderland Museum & Art Gallery Pictures

Page 30 bottom, 63 top, 106, 107 bottom, 115 top.

MERRY CHRISTMAS

Christmas Day In The Workhouse … Cinderella & Prince Charming … Christmas On The Barbary Coast … Santa's Grotto … A Christmas Carol … A Gift From Norway …

Local children pay a visit to Father Christmas in the 1950s.

Christmas Day In The Workhouse

Christmas Day in Sunderland Workhouse in 1896 started with children going through the different parts of the building singing carols. The inmates were given gifts of oranges, apples, sweets and nuts. The children had their Christmas dinner of roast beef and plum pudding separate from the adults in the schoolroom. The Mayor, businessmen and traders all donated gifts: Thomas William Backhouse gave a Christmas tree, Sunderland Co-operative Society gave fourteen 7lb boxes of sweets and others contributed boxes of oranges, books, dolls and toys.

Full House

On Christmas Day 1878 there were 740 paupers in Sunderland Workhouse – a good proportion of whom were children.

An advert for a Sunderland store at Christmas 1916.

Christmas Past

Well off individuals did their bit to help those in need at Christmas time. On 19th December 1878 John Wilson of The Green treated 136 of the very poorest children at Moor Street School to a dinner.

Christmas Break

In 1842 a Report on the Employment of Children around the country included interviews with children working at Bishopwearmouth Iron Works. Fourteen-year-old John Nicholson revealed he worked 12 hour days collecting old iron, rings, keys and binding them into bundles. At Christmas he got two or three days holiday away from the hard toil at the works.

Christmas Cheer

ROBINSON'S LANE RAGGED SCHOOLS. – The teachers of the school gave 45 of the boys a supper on Monday evening the 18th December, after which about 50 quarts of soup were distributed to the poor in the neighbourhood. The teachers held their annual tea on Christmas Day, when it was stated that since these schools were opened on September 6th, 1846, 271 scholars had been admitted, and that the children had bought by subscriptions, 28 Bibles, 27 Testaments, 54 Hymn and Prayer Books. A Clothing and Funeral Fund has also been established for their benefit.

Sunderland Herald
29th December 1848

Children enjoying their Christmas Party at Christ Church Sunday School in 1954 were paid a surprise visit by the stars of the pantomime Cinderella. Prince Charming (Ann Hart) and Cinderella (Heather Furnell) were taking a break from the Sunderland Empire where they were appearing over Christmas.

An illustration by Arthur Rackham at the turn of the century.

Stocking Filler

Between the wars large families in the East End and Hendon had little spare money to spend on Christmas presents. Kids got a stocking filled with an apple, orange, nuts and perhaps a small toy.

Lily Turnbull

Different in the '30s

In the '30s Christmas was not the same as it is now. There just wasn't the money about then. Kids were lucky to get an apple or an orange and some nuts on Christmas Day.

John Ryan

Orphan Asylum Treat

Christmas for boys in the Orphan Asylum in the East End was a special occasion. Local businessmen and shopkeepers donated money and goods to the institution at this time. On Christmas Day 1905 each boy received: a shilling, a spiced loaf, biscuits, cakes, fruit and nuts. On Boxing Day the boys were given sixpence each by another well-wisher.

Christmas on the Barbary Coast

After the war I lived with my family in Mulgrave Street, Monkwearmouth.

Nobody had much in those days. There was a tap in the yard for drinking water and this often froze in wintertime.

At Christmas we got a stocking filled with nuts, an orange, an apple, a small toy like a mouth organ and a shilling piece. Although this might not seem much to kids today, to us Christmas was a brilliant time.

Billy Dent

Christmas Day 1945

The wireless was an important form of family entertainment at this time. Programmes on Christmas Day included:

Home Service
Carols
Children's Hour

Light Programme
Family Favourites
Just William

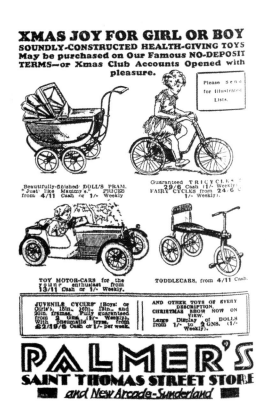

An advert for Palmer's showing
children's toys at Christmas 1935 .

Sarah Taylor with her doll and pram
in Brandling Street in 1924.

Above & right: Doreen Tindle playing
with toys in Duke Street North, Roker
in the '30s.

A certificate awarded to a local schoolgirl for helping to send Christmas parcels to servicemen overseas in 1915.

Above and left: Christmas celebrations at St Columba's, from 1893 (above) and from 1917.

Christmas Day 1950

Although there had been television transmissions from before the war few people at this time had TV sets.

Home Service
Christmas Day in the Morning
Children's Hour
Children Singing of Christmas

Margaret Watts in the Co-op store in Green Street, Christmas 1949.

Norma Johnson dressed up for a concert organised by Greta Thirkle at the Ebenezer Church in Roker Avenue in 1941.

Carol singers at the Wheatsheaf in the late 1960s.

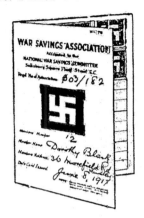
An advert from the *Sunderland Daily Echo* of 18th December 1917 encouraging children to do their bit for the war effort at Christmas. At this time the swastika was the symbol of good luck until the Nazis gave it a new meaning.

John Price on his rocking horse, *circa* 1939.

Christmas Day 1955

Home Service
Children's Hour
Light Programme
Hancock's Half Hour

BBC TV
A Christmas Visit to Disneyland
Watch With Mother

Television received a major boost to sales with the Coronation in 1953, but Radio still dominated the air waves at this time.

Although Independent Television began broadcasting in September 1955, Tyne Tees Television did not start transmissions until January 1959.

An advert from Christmas 1955 shows children's toys had to keep pace with new technology. Alongside cowboy outfits were space suits.

Four-year-old Billy Brewster in his cowboy suit in 1958.

Above: Linda Brown on her tricycle in Fell Road, Ford Estate, around 1954.

Left: June Martin on a tricycle in Dock Street in 1951.

Every boy's dream of a Christmas present in the old days – this train set belonged to young Stephen Bell's grandad.

Christmas Day 1960

BBC TV

Christmas Day in the Morning, Carols in English and Welsh

The Adventures of Hiram Holliday

Wells Fargo

Billy Smart's Circus

ITV

The One O'clock Show

Grand Christmas Circus from Glasgow

Alice Through the Looking Glass with Spike Milligan and Bernard Bresslaw

A Christmas Party in Thomas Street Junior School Hall, about 1955. This was organised by senior citizens for the children of Monkwearmouth.

EVERYTHING FOR CHRISTMAS at Liverpool House

Santa's Grotto

I remember Santa's Christmas Grotto at Liverpool House when growing up in the 1960s. It was situated in the basement of the old store in High Street. They had a different theme every year – they were great.

Richie Ankers

Family Tradition

My mam used to take me and my sister Pat to see Santa's Grotto at Liverpool House in the '50s. Years later this was one of the places I took my children, Andrew and Paula. I used to take them to every Santa in town – Joplings, Blacketts, Binns as well as those in Newcastle.

Pauline Clark

Christmas 1964

Christmas 1965

Victoria and Peter Gibson and their dog Shep in the back garden of 39 Burntland Avenue, Southwick in the mid 1980s. Snowmen sightings in Sunderland are becoming less and less common with the milder winters of recent years.

Dickens at Christmas

At Christmas time at Commercial Road Juniors in the early 1960s I remember the Headteacher Mr Tate would read Dickens' classic *A Christmas Carol* to us in the school hall. Years later I discovered Alf Tate had been a prisoner of the Japanese during the Second World War. He was serving with the 125th Anti-Tank Regiment when Singapore fell. After the war he taught at Havelock Juniors before moving on to Commercial Road.

Jackie Turnbull

Christmas Tips

When I worked on a milk round in the late 1960s and early '70s Christmas was the best time of the year. We would get around £100 each in Christmas tips. This was a fortune at the time.

Richie Ankers

Christmas Day 1965

BBC TV

Leslie Crowther Meets the Kids in Hospital

Billy Smart's Circus

Disney Time

Mother Goose Pantomime

Dr Who

BBC 2 had started the previous year but there were no Christmas programmes.

ITV

Children's Carol Service from Hexham Abbey

Lost in Space

The Beverley Hillbillies

The day ended with a festive episode of The Avengers – Too Many Christmas Trees.

Valley Rd. School
Sunderland.

Dear Aubrey,

we hope you will
get better soon
we have been doing
some exciting
things while youve
been away we have
had a bring and buy
sale to make
money for our
christmas party we
have had anopen
day when some
peoples mothers came
to look at our work

we have had a nuse
who came to look
at our teeth we
have been making
animals of long ago
out of clay
we will be soon
a play for practising
we hope you will
soon be Back to
School

love from Ib

A letter from 1b at Valley Road School to their classmate Aubrey Harvey who was in hospital with inflammation of the hip in 1962. The class reported on what he was missing as Christmas approached.

A nativity play staged by pupils of Hasting Hill in 1993.

Children at Hasting Hill staging their Christmas Play in the early 1980s. Generation after generation of Sunderland schoolchildren have played their part in this annual celebration. From Angels to Wise Men, from Mary and Joseph to the Shepherds, in the eyes of watching parents *their* child is the star of the show.

Christmas Day 1970

BBC 1

Rolf Harris Meets the Kids in Hospital

Basil Brush

Billy Smart's Circus

Disney World

Robinson Crusoe Pantomime

BBC 2

Play School

ITV

Thunderbirds

Flipper

Kelvin Hall Circus

Cinderella

On the Buses

A Gift From Norway

In December 1962 the people of Stavanger in Norway sent a giant Christmas tree to the people of Sunderland. The 40 feet tall tree was erected in Mowbray Terrace and on the 18th December the Mayors of both towns were present when the lights were turned on. Stavanger's Mayor, Mr Jan Johnson, said, 'Oslo sends its tree to London, Bergen sends one to Newcastle and now Stavanger sends one to Sunderland, so the three most important places in Norway send gifts to the three most important places in England'. A choir of sixty children from Redby Boys' School and West Park Girls' Technical School sang carols at the ceremony.

SECTION TWO

FUN AND GAMES

Gambling On The Moor ... Middleton Camp ... Girls' Guildry ... Boys' Brigade ... The Circus Comes To Town ... Quatermass & The Kid ...

Hill View Juniors netball team, 1955-56.

John George Brown, aged 3 in 1917, with clay pipe to blow bubbles. The pose was in the style of Millais' painting *Bubbles* made famous in the Pears Soap advert. Young John grew up to be a River Wear foyboatman.

Margaret Watts in the back lane of Victor Street with her nephew in 1960.

Sarah Taylor on milk float horse Mattie at stables near the Fulwell Mill in the 1920s. On the right is her uncle Percy Arthur whose round covered Fulwell, Roker and Seaburn.

Children take a break from their game of cricket outside The Neptune public house in Woodbine Street East in the 1930s. Front row, left to right: Billy Rudd, Florrie Cowie, ? Newby, Tommy Leathead. Back row: Billy Henry, Walter Martin.

Wash Day and Bath Day

The families who shared our building in Mulgrave Street also shared one wash house, this meant they had different wash days. After my mother finished washing the hot water was not wasted because we got in the poss tub for a bath.

Billy Dent

Doreen Tindle is dwarfed by the poss stick and wash tub in a back yard in Duke Street North in 1931.

Children playing on top of an early washing machine in the back yard of 95 Victor Street in 1956.

Gambling on the Sabbath

On Sunday 10th May 1840, thirteen-year-old boat builder James Murphy of Hedworth Street was caught gambling in Vine Street, Monkwearmouth Shore, during divine service.

A week later another boat builder, fourteen-year-old John Cowley, was charged with gambling on the Hetton Railway at Bishopwearmouth during divine service. The charge against both boys was dropped.

Gambling on the Moor

A Commission of clergy and laymen produced a Report in November 1896 on the conditions of life in Sunderland's East End. Those providing evidence included, schoolteachers, medical men and Relieving Officers.

One of the things they found was that 90% of people in the area indulged in betting. 'It is by no means confined to the adult population, but is engaged in quite generally by girls and boys in their teens. Some bookmakers will take bets of one penny from children. Another witness, crossing the Moor on a Sunday saw no less than four groups engaged in pitch-and-toss, and two seats occupied by card players; a third witness, well able to judge, asserted that the arithmetic of scholars who have passed out of the Public Elementary Schools was mostly kept up by the calculation of odds'.

Sisters, Sarah (with doll) and Anne Taylor at Netherburn Road in 1927. After the First World War the Taylor family lived in four upstairs rooms at 6 Brandling Street and they had their name down on the Council waiting list for years. Shortly after receiving news that they would get a house in newly built Netherburn Road, Mrs Taylor died. Mr Taylor decided that he and his five sons and four daughters would still make the move. Twenty years later Sarah was married with her own child – one-year-old Peter (*pictured above right*) in the back yard of his home in Gray Street, Hendon in 1948. The toddler is standing on a cracket and had been playing with coke seen scattered around the yard.

SCHOOLS HOLIDAY CAMP, MIDDLETON-IN-TEESDALE. 90649 JV

Middleton Camp in Teesdale will be remembered by thousands of Wearsiders who stayed there during their schooldays. The camp opened on 8th April 1922, the hall and adjoining field had been purchased for £900 the previous year with the approval of the Education Committee.

The first school parties to book in were Ryhope Secondary and the Junior Technical School at Easter 1922. They were followed by James William Street Boys, Moor Boys, Diamond Hall Girls and Stansfield Street Girls.

During the Second World War Middleton Camp was requisitioned by the military for internment purposes.

Children from Castle View, Redby and Bishop Harland schools at Middleton Camp in May 1979.

Sunderland Boys 1906-07. Back row (boys only): Lamb, Abbot, Warren. Middle row: Forster, Musgrave, Stanley, Hunter. Front row: S. Bainbridge, Thomson, Greaves, A. Bainbridge. Hanson.

Sunderland Boys, winners of the English Schools' Shield in 1933. Back row, left to right: Tony Minchella (St Patrick's), William Connor (Redby), Ray Middleton (Boldon), Arthur Storey (Ryhope), Allenby Chilton (Ford), Tommy Maughan (West Park). Front row: Arnold Lowes (Castletown), George Turnbull (Monkwearmouth Central), Billy Robinson (Whitburn), Ernie Forrest (Hudson Road), John Dryden (West Park). Nine of the team went on to sign for League clubs.

Boys' Club

After the Skiff Inn, Beach Street, closed as a public house in 1936 it opened as a boys' club the following year. In the early years times were hard and it was difficult to collect the penny a week subscription from the boys.

At the outbreak of the war ex-Royal Navy man Tom Retford took charge of the club. Interior walls were knocked down to allow room for a table tennis table to be installed. Boxing and football were popular activities organised by the club. A library was set up with the help of a Carnegie grant.

When the Skiff Boys' Club celebrated its tenth anniversary in 1947 it could boast a membership of 75 with a long waiting list. The former pub turned boys' club disappeared in the clearances and redevelopment of Deptford.

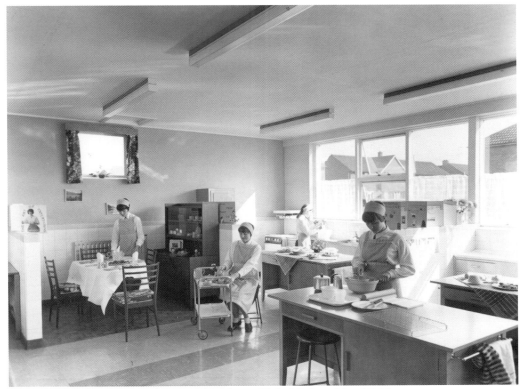

A cookery class at St Thomas Aquinas Girls' School in 1964.

Members of the Girls' Guildry, Dock Street Methodist Church.

The Girls' Guildry was founded in 1900 in Scotland to provide opportunities for Christian girls to serve the community. In 1965 the Girls' Guildry was amalgamated with the Girls' Brigade.

Certificate of Admittance to the Girls' Guildry.

Good Friday marchers in Forster Street in 1960 with Girls' Guildry leaders Miss Lautebach and Miss Cuthbert.

The twenty first anniversary of the Girls' Guildry, Dock Street Methodist Church, Monkwearmouth, 1960. Back row, left to right: Margaret Downes, Dorothy Thompson, Joyce Beaton, Celia Jackson, Phylis Lee, Brenda Hudson, Mary Wallace, Margaret Steabler. Middle row: Linda Dodds, Margaret Watts, Alice Lautebach, Hetty Cuthbert, Linda Hanbury, Norma Sanderson. Front row: Joan Davidson, Nancy McDermont, Margaret Clarke, Joan Weston, Brenda Atkinson, Linda Jackson.

The end of the 1960 Good Friday parade in Forster Street.

Right: Everybody wanted to be a star but the Beatles beat them to it. Left to right: Kevin Fairclough, Les West and John McDermott in a Square off Galashields Road, Grindon, *circa* 1966.

Below: Hill View Jazz Band. The 1960s was the heyday of Jazz Bands. They were very popular with children in Sunderland and surrounding neighbourhood.

Left: Southmoor School Brass Band with Mr Hudson (conductor) and PE teacher Mr Watt (trumpet), *circa* 1961. They had the distinction of being the first Sunderland school to take part in the British Brass Band Finals (Junior section). Southmoor came fourth in the Finals at Belle Vue, Manchester.

Top 40

When we lived at Devonshire Street near the Wheatsheaf in the '60s I remember Sunday was always a quiet day. Kids only had school to look forward to the following day. One of the lads used to let us listen to the Top 40 hit records in his dad's car which was parked outside his house.

Graham Brown

Budding Stars

When I was about fourteen in 1965 I used to go to see groups play at Grindon Congregational Church Hall. One band had a young drummer from High Barnes called Nigel Olsson, who went on to play for Elton John for many years. Another budding star was guitarist Mick Grabham from Grindon, who went on to play in Plastic Penny and later joined Procol Harum.

Geoff Pearson

Rawhide

In the early sixties my two sisters used to get the latest pop records. I remember my first record – *Rawhide* by Frankie Laine. I think my sisters bought it for my birthday.

Jackie Turnbull

Right: Violinists accompanied by the percussion section at Redby School in 1979.

Boys' Brigade

The Boys' Brigade was founded by William Alexander Smith in Glasgow in 1883. Its aim was to fill the gap for boys who were getting too big for Sunday School but not old enough to join the YMCA (at 17 years old).

The Object of the Brigade was 'the advancement of Christ's Kingdom among Boys, and the promotion of habits of Obedience, Reverence, Discipline, Self-Respect, and all that tends towards a true Christian Manliness'.

Right: A Boys' Brigade (Dock Street Methodists) membership card from 1961-62. At this time the Brigade had a worldwide membership of 156,000 with another 86,000 in the junior reserve.

Below: Members of Southwick Boys' Brigade assemble at Sunderland Railway Station to travel to the annual camp, *circa* 1951.

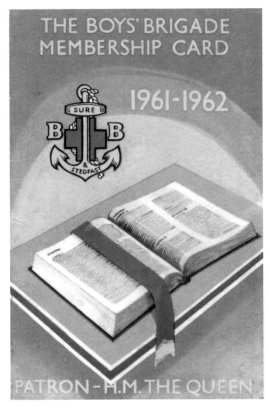

Under the Bonfire

Around the 1963/64 period slum houses were being demolished all round the Wheatsheaf area. These stretches of land awaiting development we called 'bombsites'. The name came from a previous generation who played on land laid waste by bombing.

On the site where Eglinton Tower multi-storey flats now stands I remember we built a massive bonfire. Guy Fawkes Night seemed to be much more of an event at that time than it is today. For weeks we would collect junk for our bonfire. By the big night it was massive and it is amazing to think now that we had a gang hut at its centre. Inside the base were old chairs and settees which we got to through a covered entrance. Everything was built around and over this 'den' until it reached a height of thirty or forty feet. Its frightening to think what might have happened if this had caught fire prematurely (not an uncommon event) when we were inside.

Colin Smith

Some of those who could not get outdoors still had the opportunity to enjoy fireworks. Nurses at Sunderland Children's Hospital put on a display for their young patients on Guy Fawkes Night 1958.

Early Bonfires

In the summer of 1841 George Burnhope (aged 11) and Henry Wood (aged 14) from Sunderland were charged with making bonfires in public streets. The charges were later discharged.

St Mary's School 'Captain Ball' team in 1922. Captain Ball was an early form of netball.

Hendon Board Boys' School rugby XV, 1949. PE teacher Jack Washington is on the right. He introduced rugby to the school after the war. Bob Storr who taught woodwork is on the left. He helped to run the team. Jack Washington recalls: 'We started the lads off playing practice games on Hendon Burn which adjoined the school. The Burn was rough ground with cinders on it etc. and it was too dangerous to allow normal tackling. So we played touch rugby which encouraged quick passing. Then we went up to play at Spark's Farm. All of the lads were very keen in those days.'

A Scottish Dancing Class at Dock Street Methodist Church in 1951. Back row, left to right: unknown, unknown, Olga Kirton, Nellie Knowles, Mary Smiles, Edna Renny. Front row: Norma Johnson, Ann Wrightson, Miriam Smiles, Eleanor Robson.

Southmoor School football team, 1962.

Dock Street Methodist Church 1950s
By Margaret Thynne

Dock Street Methodist Church was a hive of activity in the late '50s with various clubs and meetings throughout the week. There was the Girls' Guildry and the Greenwoods on Monday evenings. Tuesday was for the Boys' Brigade and also the Christian Endeavour for the adults. There was a Young Ladies' Guild and a Ropery Girls' Guild. The Ropery girls purchased the wooden clock which was in the main gallery of the church. Fridays would be for choir practice or concert parties and the church also had a Drama Club which was enjoyed by all. Regular bazaars were held in the junior rooms.

Every Sunday afternoon children ranging from three to fifteen could be seen making their way towards Dock Street for Sunday School meetings at the church. The church also looked after the children through the week; there was the Girls' Guildry for the older girls and the Greenwoods for younger children. The ladies who took charge of the girls were Miss A. Lautebach and Miss H. Cuthbert, Mrs Learmouth also helped teach the girls Scottish dancing. There were trips to different places to compete with other troops. The badge which was worn by the Guild was an oil lamp and the motto was 'Wise unto that which is good'. Certificates could be gained in First Aid, Manners and Customs and Religious Knowledge.

Sunday School treats were looked forward to by everyone, even the mothers. The church would organise outings to various places, such as Lumley Castle, Saltwell Park or Crimdon Dene. These trips were the only time some of the children ever got to venture from the area.

Harvest Festival at Dock Street Methodist Church in 1951.

Harvest Festivals were a time for celebration and the children were given a little verse to learn to recite in the church in front of the congregation. At Christmas time there were parties for all, everyone would receive a paper bag full of treats. Games were played in the big hall at the back of the church.

Scripture exams were enjoyed by all and on week days after school Miss Hetty Cuthbert would invite everyone to her little cottage in Forster Street where we were taught the scriptures. The house would be full of children. This kept everyone busy and took thoughts of hanging around street corners out of their minds. Remember, not everyone had television sets in those days. Miss Hetty had a heart of gold and everyone loved her.

Right: A trip to Lumley Castle in 1954. Left to right: Linda Hanbury, Robert Day and Margaret Watts.

Lumley Castle, 1953. Mrs Watts and Mrs Porteous are in the centre of the group.

Comic Wars

When I was growing up in the '60s I used to get the *Victor* and *Hotspur* comics. Characters like Alf Tupper 'The Tough of the Track' appeared every week. Many of the stories were about warfare. There was Braddock VC the flying ace and V for Vengeance about a suicide squad in the last war. Years later when I had grown up my nephew used to get the *Warlord*. I looked at this one day and was interested to see a serial about a German soldier. This being the late '70s the Cold War was at its height and the cartoon character's enemy was not British but Russian. He was seen fighting on the Russian Front and avoiding the tricky problem of killing British soldiers.

Tommy Johnson

Above: A copy of *The Hotspur* from 1954.

Right: An advert from the *Echo* for the first edition of the girls' magazine *School Friend* which came out on 11th May 1950.

Joyce Beaton winning a race at the TLF Sports Centre around 1949. The TLF (Thompson/Laing/Forge) stood near the old Redby School off Fulwell Road.

Sunderland Boys line up at Ryhope Colliery Welfare ground in December 1962, before they beat Stockton Boys in the English Schools' Trophy.

Above: Members of Grangetown Swimming Club in the 1950s.

Right: A family enjoy a trip to Newcastle Road Baths shortly after its opening. The Mayor, Thomas Summerbell performed the opening ceremony on 3rd June 1936.

Below: Girls at St Thomas Aquinas School Baths in the 1960s.

Swimming & Football

When the Mayor opened Newcastle Road Baths he said 'Sunderland lagged far behind many inland towns so far as swimming facilities were concerned. In Lancashire towns, for instance, swimming was carried on with almost the same enthusiasm that football aroused in Sunderland'.

With the opening of the new Baths he hoped the swimmers of Sunderland would take a bigger pride in their art and make a name for Sunderland as a swimming town as well as a football town.

St Hilda's Junior School football team in 1961-62 season. Back row, left to right: Neil Kibble, Arthur Milligan, Andrew Metcalfe, Michael Ellison, Vincent Lynch. Front row: Anthony Truman, Robert Healey, Trevor Regan, Peter Gibson, John Watters. There are only ten boys in the picture because the captain Davie Medcalf slept in on the morning the photograph was taken.

Havelock Juniors football team, 1955-56. While swimming has become an increasingly popular sport and pastime on Wearside, Sunderland is still very much a football 'town'.

West Park netball team, 1958.

NATIONAL SAVINGS
STAMP BOOK

THE STAMPS IN THIS BOOK SHOULD BE USED FOR

DEPOSITING IN		BUYING
POST OFFICE SAVINGS BANK	OR FOR	NATIONAL SAVINGS CERTIFICATES
TRUSTEE SAVINGS BANKS		DEFENCE BONDS

PLEASE DO NOT STICK STAMPS OF DIFFERENT VALUES ON THE SAME SHEET

National Savings stamp books were a popular way of saving for children. Sixpence (2$\frac{1}{2}$p) was the value of one of the stamps.

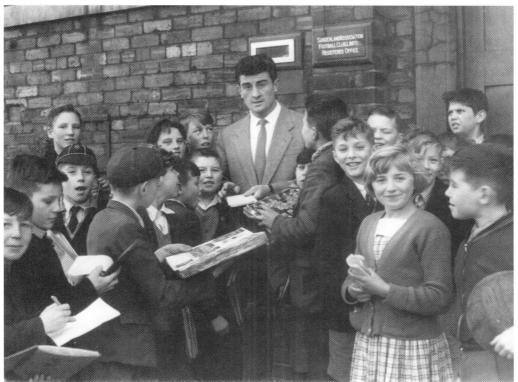

Charlie Hurley is besieged by autograph hunters outside Roker Park shortly after his signing in October 1957. The boy third from the left with the cub cap is Les Herbert. In the past, as is the case today, footballers have been heroes to thousands of Sunderland youngsters.

Bede football team, Town Champions, 1961-62. When the teacher saw Les Herbert (second from left, back row) he told him off for 'showing bare acres of chest'.

Hylton Road football team, 1951-52 season. Fred Wright is second from left, front row.

Above: Hylton Castle Junior School cricket team in the 1950s.

Right: A member of Redby cricket team between the wars – cricket kit was always in short supply.

Keep Off The Path

Skating and sliding on the footpath in Sunderland was an activity that could land you in court in the 1840s.

Ten days before Christmas 1840 Thomas Monroe (aged 13) and John Wilson (aged 13) were charged with skating on the footpaths in Union Street and Bridge Street respectively.

A couple of weeks later Robert Rimington (aged 10) of Spring Garden Lane, David Rutherford (aged 12) of Grey Street and George Marshall (aged 12) of Vine Street were all arrested for sliding on the footpath. All three East End children were discharged.

Youngsters on the frozen boating lake in Roker Park in January 1958.

Freezing Swim

The area of land between Grindon Lane and Goldsmith Road that is now part of Barnes Park extension was once both a playground and a wonderful place teeming with trees and wildlife and adventure. In bad weather the Grindon side used to flood, as it was fed by streams – rain and melted snow. We would often walk home from Broadway Junior School this way – playing in Grindon Park then cutting across the open field. Until one day we got there and it was totally flooded – and I mean flooded. The Fire Brigade was there trying to pump the floodwater away. So we went to walk around. But one lad – Eddie Barnes was his name – stripped down to his underpants, walked down the bank and dived in. And YES he swam right across – memory can distort things, but I swear he must have swam at least 75 yards! We were so busy watching him nobody thought to pick up his clothes, so when he had finished he had to run back around, soaking wet and freezing, to get them.

Geoff Pearson

Above: Southmoor School athletics team, 1962.

A number of schools used to hold their Sports Day at Spark's Farm on Hill View Estate. In 1971 Wearside College of Further Education was built on the site.

Right: Members of Thorney Close School athletics team in 1981.

Below: Long jumping at Thornhill School.

A game of rounders in Chester Road School yard in the late '70s.

St Patrick's Junior School football team, 1957-58 season.

Scary Amusement

Growing up in the 1950s my mother used to take me to department stores like Joplings and Liverpool House. I remember both these shops had their own money, some of the coins had holes in the middle. In Joplings shoe department there was an X-ray machine through which you saw the bones in your feet.

Geoff Pearson

An advert from the *Echo* for Joplings' Sunderland store in June 1950.

Savage Amusement

A Report to the Board of Health on Sunderland published in 1851 revealed that seeing animals being slaughtered in the street was a common sight even for children.

Mr Kidson said that in front of the shop in Sans Street he had counted as many as thirty or forty children, amusing themselves by looking at a poor animal being knocked down and getting its throat cut, which he did not think could have a very humanizing tendency.

A class at Redby show off their Halloween lanterns in the mid '70s – a less scary activity for kids.

Born in Backhouse Park

I was born at ten past midnight on 18th April 1946 in Backhouse Park. My parents lived in a Royal Air Force wooden Nissen hut.

They had lived there for about 18 months before I was born. The hut had been used by air and army personnel during the war when a barrage balloon had been anchored in the park.

My mother said the summers were great but the winters were very bleak – even the hot water bottles froze.

Our house was near the swings and roundabouts at the Cedars end of the park. My older brother Derek and sister Marjorie have told me stories of how good it was sledging in the winter down the banks from our house. In the summertime they had smashing picnics.

As far as we are aware I am the only person legally born in Backhouse Park. We lived there till I was three years old. Not everyone had a back garden so big.

Eileen Herbert (née Hedley)

Young Eileen Hedley in Backhouse Park in 1947.

Lads enjoy the snow on Mowbray Park in the 1950s. The picture is taken from Toward Road looking across Park Road.

A balaclava helps Billy Brewster keep warm on the beach at Roker in 1959.

Ann and Joyce Henderson and their cousin Anne Wilson playing in rock pools in the early '50s.

Jack and Leslie Brown playing on the beach at Seaburn in 1926.

Plodging at Roker before the First World War.

Youngsters play around the Holey Rock in the 1930s.

The Reay family enjoying a day on the beach at Seaburn in August 1951.

Youngsters enjoying traditional Sports Day games at Hasting Hill School in 1992.

A class at the old Redby School working with seaweed gathered from the beach.

The Circus Comes To Town

After the last war huge crowds used to turn out to see the circus procession to Seaburn. The elephants would lead the way from Monkwearmouth Station, past the Wheatsheaf, down Roker Avenue and along the seafront.

Local shops would put up circus posters in return for a couple of free tickets. After the circus had gone I used to get the poster from a shopkeeper every year. I kept these for years before throwing the whole collection out.

Billy Dent

Elephants from Bertram Mills Circus leaving Monkwearmouth Railway Station in June 1950. Youngsters packed the route on their way to the Big Top at Seaburn.

Left: In July 1966 a bowling competition for youngsters was held at the Bowling Alley in Newcastle Road. At this time a bowling league was held each Saturday morning for children. The Bowling Alley had opened in the summer of 1964 and cost £300,000 to build.

Brownies meet the Mayor of Sunderland, Councillor Len Harper in 1980.

Monkwearmouth All Saints Church football team in 1960-61 season.

Quatermass and the Kid

By Geoff Pearson

As we grow up we must all have certain memories, things we would rather forget, or rather *other* people would forget! The silly things you've done in life – those embarrassing moments when you felt like dying. Well two of my early episodes had to do with one other person – Margie Toomey.

Growing up at Grindon in the '50s, most of the other kids I knew were friends of my sister who is five years older than me. So it follows so were most of her friends. I was at the time about five years old and the said Miss Toomey would have been a sophisticated lady of eight or nine and of course I was absolutely in love. Anyway the time came for Margie to have a birthday party and we were all invited. It was either a Saturday or Sunday afternoon – Sunday I think, so off we went. It was a smashing party – lots of jelly and cakes and pop 'n stuff, games and presents, what have you. Then some smart Alec had the bright idea to turn

The Grindon Village Kid – Geoff Pearson circa 1956.

on the TV so that they didn't miss the latest episode of the serial they had been following. So we quietened down and gathered around the set as it warmed up ready to entertain us. THEN on IT came, the latest episode of Quatermass (and the Pit)! I was off, I dived behind the couch screaming and wouldn't come out. Well they didn't know whether to watch the TV or spend their time laughing at me. Meanwhile I was terrified to look at the TV. So my ever understanding and compassionate sister Liz went and told my mum in between screams of laughter. So mum came and rescued her little boy and took him home so the rest of the kids could watch Quatermass in peace. Well for a week or two afterwards I didn't feel like playing outside, much to the delight of my sister.

But it doesn't end there though. True love will survive, so about two years later (it was New Year's Eve) I had to try to impress Margie. The grown-ups were indoors and all us kids were playing on an ice slide outside on Galashields Road bank. It was a real belter too – really slippery! Now Margie was a bit timid about the slide, so I thought I would come to her rescue and give her a hand – just a little push to get her started.

So when they brought her back from hospital with her leg broken that was when I think I realised this wasn't meant to be! Then the next summer off she went to Bede School – the seniors! Well that was that then. She now works at Sunderland Royal Hospital, probably just as well if she has any grown up friends like me!

Yes those were the days.

Michael Lowes (left) and brother Fred *circa* 1960. Dressed like 'old men' but aged around 11 and 12 years old.

Lifeboys outside Dock Street Flats in the mid 1960s.

The front of the Roker End was a prime site for young supporters in the 1960s. As they grew up they took their place further back on the terraces.

Countryside on the Doorstep
By Irene Gibson

I moved from the slums of Hendon, where I was born in 1951, into a new modern 3 bedroom house in Pennywell, when I was only 3 months old. My parents took me out into the surrounding countryside regularly. I witnessed the changing scenes. I can remember standing where Grindon is now and gazing into the distance towards Penshaw and as far as I could see was a patch-work quilt made up of farmland. Browns, greens and yellow mingled together to create the landscape.

My favourite walk was to the Blue Bell Woods behind Penshaw Monument. My mam thought the fresh air would benefit me, because I was recovering from scarlet fever. When we neared the woods I could smell the familiar fragrance of wild onions. Then I would stand still, amazed at the sight before me, a mass of sweet smelling blue flowers swaying in the breeze. I always remember the blue bells being tall, as a small child they were up to my knees. My mam would help me pick them and she would fill my arms. I still love these flowers and when I look at them I return to Blue Bell Woods and see my mam's smiling face.

I now work in a school at Pennywell as a nursery nurse. I told the children at story-time about Blue Bell Woods and that I loved the flower. The next day, a little boy brought a present for me. It was a blue bell. He said to me: 'It's because it's your best flower'.

Irene Gibson (third from right in the front row) at Barnes School, circa 1960.

I went to Barnes School and the parents of many of the other children in my class were well off. I remember we could take in biscuits to have with our morning milk. My classmates used to take in chocolate biscuits, some of them had chocolate teacakes in foil wrappers which looked really posh. I used to take a digestive biscuit in a brown paper bag. I used to keep the bag in my pocket and take a few crumbs out at a time. My mam always used to do the best she could but we just didn't have the money.

Childhood Memories of the 'Back of the Pit'
By Margaret Thynne

When I was growing up in the 1950s and early '60s my grandparents, Alfred and Elizabeth Stead, lived at the 'Back of the Pit', Monkwearmouth. This small community of about eight streets lay between Wearmouth Bridge and where Sunderland's Stadium of Light stands today.

There were three shops in Brooke Street. On one corner was Meggie Rowe's general dealers. Meggie was a small black haired woman who wore gold earrings and always had a cheerful smile. Opposite Meggie's was a fish shop and a few doors down from this was Billy Cutter's little shop – it was his front room. The counter was small and the room was dark and sparse. The front window was an ordinary front room window with small boxes of sweets and chocolates tightly squeezed together. I liked Billy; he was kind and considerate to small children and of course I loved to buy sweets there.

The Stead children: Maud (left), Peter and Elizabeth (Libby) outside a pub in Brooke Street in the late '30s.

Mothers and children in Wilson Street after the war.

Kids in Hay Street in the 1950s.

Over the bank top was a great place to play, this led to the 'Runner' which in turn led to the Wharf down by the riverside. We were not supposed to go down there because there were incidents of children falling into the river and drowning.

On the corner of Wreath Quay Road and Hay Street was Frankie Wiehl's shop. Frankie was short-tongued and always wore a beret. I also liked Frankie, and this was another good shop for sweets – especially ice cream. I can still picture him reaching down into that large freezer of his.

When I was about six years old I was walking over the Wreath Quay bank when a bull escaped on its way to the slaughterhouse near the Wheatsheaf. Luckily the bull ran off in the other direction down Roker Avenue.

The children in the area went to: Thomas Street School, Colliery School and St Benet's Roman Catholic School.

Sarah Allen used to run trips for people living at the back of the pit. *Right*: This one was probably at Saltwell Park. Standing, left to right: Joan Sopp, unknown, Pat Brown. Peeping behind: Barbara Potts and Tony Thompson. Sitting: Billy Curry, Alfie Stead, Irene Mooney, Kathy Boothe, Jean Brown, Robert Brown, Marjorie Brown.

Children gather around the traffic policeman at the Wheatsheaf in an era of boys in short trousers and girls in ankle socks.

Children in Moorgate Street during the East End Carnival in 1912.

Moorgate Street

When I was growing up in the 1930s we lived in Moorgate Street down the East End. There were two families living upstairs and two down in our building. The Moor Board School was out the back and the lads there used to jump over the wall and go through our yard. When we moved across the street to Number 31 I couldn't believe we had our own bath.

The East End always made a big thing of Royal occasions like Coronations. This was especially true of Moorgate Street, which was always praised for its decorations. I remember one bloke used to dress up as Gandhi.

John Ryan

SECTION THREE

LITTLE 'UNS
AT WORK

Young Iron Workers ... Runaway Apprentices ... Gleaning Potatoes ... Milk Round Early Start ... Golf Caddie ... Logan's Run ...

A class in Sunderland Blind School in the 1930s. The Local Education Authority had a responsibility to give blind children vocational training for life after school. Crafts taught included: basket-making, machine knitting, chair caning and bed and mattress making.

Young Workers in the Nineteenth Century

In 1842 a Report on the Employment of Children in the region was published. One of those who collected evidence for the Report was J.R. Leifchild. Among those he interviewed were children working at Bishopwearmouth Iron Works. He found the witnesses seemingly healthy but very ragged and dirty:

No. 588. — *John Grahams.*
Aged 12; carries flats (flat bars) to the warehouse; is only just come here. Cannot spell, read, or write. Was learning a b c's at a day school, when he came away. Lives with his parents; sometimes goes to Sunday school, and sometimes to church.

No. 589. — *Abraham Thompson.*
Ten years old. Hooks up the iron that goes through the rolling-mills. Comes to work at 5 o'clock A.M., and goes away at sometimes 6 or 7 at night. Gets 5s a-week. Gets his meals when he has time. Cannot read, or spell, or write.

No. 590. — *George Hardy.*
Aged 15. Strikes with the hammer that beats out the puddlers' tools. Works from 6 A.M. to 6 P.M. Lives with his parents, and goes home to meals. Goes to no school in the week, but goes to Sunday school. Many of the boys idle about on Sundays, playing mischief and gaping eggs (a sort of game in which one boy tries to break the egg that another holds in his hand). Most of the boys here are healthy, but they are bad boys, and always fighting and stealing; two were fighting this morning at breakfast-time. They swear a vast. Witness goes to the Methodist chapel and school on Sunday. Never sees the boys beat much. One man, who minds the scrap lads, who has a wooded leg, about a week ago struck a lad with a broom-shank across the sides, and the boy tumbled down and could not speak for ever so long. The man was taken before the justice, and had to pay the lad's wages for 3 weeks, and the doctor's bill and all. This is an uncommon case. Scrap-boys are the worst boys, the worst off, and the worst used.

Runaways

In the last century boys were apprenticed to local tradesmen and girls placed in domestic service from as young as 10 years of age. Right up to the First World War there were more girls in domestic service than any other single occupation.

In 1869 the Poor Law Commission estimated four out of every five girls and boys put into service or apprenticeship failed and led to the children becoming vagrants or destitute on the streets.

Many found themselves in trouble with the law when they tried to leave their employment.

On 22nd June 1840 chain maker John Gilhespie (aged 12) was charged with running away from Booth & Co, Chain & Anchor Smiths, Monkwearmouth Shore. On the same day rope maker Thomas Bacon (aged 14) ran away from John Hay, Rope Maker of Monkwearmouth. The charge against both was dropped.

In the following months more boys were charged with absenting themselves. Eleven-year-old tailor William Airson ran away from the services of Matthew Campbell. Shoe maker John Little (aged 10) had the additional charge of stealing and destroying his indentures laid against him.

John Needham (aged 12) an apprentice boat builder was charged with absenting himself from his master Mr M. Wake of Barclay Street, Monkwearmouth Shore on 11th November 1840. The charge was dropped when he promised to go back to his employment.

On 15th November 1840 chimney sweep John Dinam (aged 14) of Union Lane was charged with absenting himself from his master. The charge was later dropped.

In 1842 it became illegal to force anyone under 21 to enter a chimney. In the same year no one under 16 could be a bound apprentice.

Sunderland Post Office Telegraph Boys, *circa* 1885. The man in the centre is Thomas Toft who was in charge of the boys.

Young miners at Wearmouth Colliery in 1918. Joe Curtis is in the front row on the right.

Working Children & The Law

In 1935 Sunderland Council published a set of Bye-Laws which listed the jobs prohibited to children (under 14 years old). These included:

• As a lather boy in a barber's or hairdresser's shop.

• In the kitchen of any hotel, cook shop, fried fish shop, eating house or ice cream saloon.

• As a marker or attendant in any billiard or bagatelle saloon.

• In connection with the sale of intoxicating liquors (except places where it is sold in sealed vessels).

• Selling programmes or refreshments in any theatre, music hall, picture theatre or other place of public entertainment.

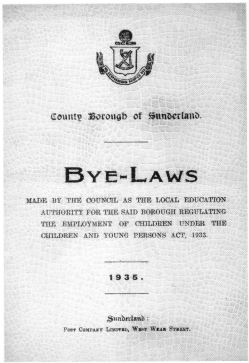

Bye-Laws covering the employment of children in Sunderland in 1935.

• In collecting or sorting rags, scrap material or refuse.

• As an attendant or assistant on a fairground for the purpose of public amusement by means of automatic machines, shooting ranges or games of skill or chance.

• In any slaughterhouse or knackers yard.

• In connection with any racing course or track.

No child could work on school days except between the hours of 5 pm and 7 pm. A child could work between 7 am and 8 am on school days delivering milk or newspapers. A child could work for no longer than five hours and not at all on Sunday.

Sunderland Mayor E.W. Ditchburn who signed the 1935 Bye-Laws.

YMCA

My mother and father worked in the YMCA in Borough Road and then in Toward Road between the wars. They started as caretakers and then became stewards.

My father fought in the First World War and was wounded in action. He was shot in the knee and had a limp for the rest of his life. He was never bitter about his injury. He used to say if he ever met the German soldier who fired the bullet he would have shaken his hand.

I used to do a number of odd jobs at the YMCA. In the '20s there was always dances or whist drives being held there. I used to watch the cloakrooms as a teenager, looking after coats at a penny a time. Sometimes women from the colliery districts like Silksworth brought their children along. The bairns would sit beside me while their mothers played whist.

I used to be sent to pay the catering bill at Notarianni's at the bottom of Silksworth Row. It was only 8/6d but the man there always gave me an ice cream cornet for nothing.

Lily Turnbull sitting with left to right: her brother Jackie, her dad, cousin Molly and Uncle Alf in the 1920s.

When I was about four or five years old my father gave me the nickname 'Tweddle'. My Uncle Arthur was a First Mate and stayed with us when home from sea. I used to say I'll clean your boots for a penny. He said I was a 'twist', so I became 'Twist Tweddle'.

Around this time I used to take empty beer bottles back to the Palatine Hotel for the penny deposit. I used to take them in a case almost as big as me. I would go in with as many as a dozen bottles. The big barman used to kid on: 'Oh, You back again?'

Lily Turnbull

Three Terraces

I started Deptford Terrace School at the end of the First World War when we lived in Glass Street. From there I went to Green Terrace School off Crowtree Road. My final school was Cowan Terrace which I joined in the spring of 1925. Three years later, a month after my fourteenth birthday, I left to start work as an assistant steward with my dad at the YMCA.

Lily Turnbull

You're never too young to start work – Jean Bruce feeding hens on Southwick Red House Farm in the late 1930s. This farm was on the site where the factory formerly known as Hepworth & Grandage now stands.

Farmers' children were expected to do their fair share of duties on the farm.

A group of Monkwearmouth lads returning from gleaning a potato field at Cleadon in October 1957. At this time sacks of potatoes were a welcome free addition to mothers' larders.

A school photograph of Aubrey Harvey at Commercial Road – the last until the war was over.

Photographers

My first job when I left school at 14 in 1939 was at Franklin's the Photographers at Bishopwearmouth. I used to cycle around the chemist shops in town and pick up spools of film in the morning. This would be developed and printed then I would drop them off at night.

When the war started photography was discouraged – you couldn't take a camera down Seaburn because people would think you were a spy. I lost my job because of this.

John Ryan

Golf Caddie

In the '60s when I was living at Town End Farm I used to caddie for golfers at Boldon Golf Club. For a round lasting over three hours we were paid 3/6d or if we were lucky five bob. Some Saturdays or Sundays we would do two rounds in a day.

Tommy Smith

Milk Round

Between 1968 and 1971 I worked on a milk round on Red House and Witherwack Estates. I used to get up at 5.30 every morning, get a quick wash, have a cup of tea and a piece of toast and leave the house for ten to six. I'd finish around 7.45 and then get ready for school. It was alright in the summer but wintertime was pretty hard. We used to get wrapped in jumpers, coats, balaclavas and gloves. Another way we kept warm was by running about.

The owner of the milk round was called Les Dodds and one of the other lads on the round was Alan 'Kit' Carson. I was about 14 when I started and the pay was £3 a week. I was pleased when I started my apprenticeship as an electrician – I got a lie-in.

Richie Ankers

A boy delivering milk in Trafalgar Square in the East End in the 1930s.

Logan's Run

As a child in the late 1940s and '50s I would collect bottles and jam jars for their penny deposit with my mates. Sometimes we would go to Sand Point where men repaired boats and we would collect copper nails they discarded. Whatever we collected we took to Logan's at the Wheatsheaf next to Thomas Street School.

The Cora.

The money we got we spent on things like going to the pictures at the Cora. The Cora only had wooden benches for seats and the owner Mrs Tindle would come round with a long hand pump and spray us with some kind of insecticide – I think it was DDT. We only went to the Roker when we were courting because that was 3d more than the Cora.

Billy Dent

Projectionist

One night in 1941 I was at the Roker Variety Theatre with my mother when a slide came up on screen. The message read: 'Boy Wanted for Projection Room.' My mother took me to the back of the theatre to see the manager Mr Clark. Although I was only thirteen years old I got the job. At the time I was at Monkwearmouth Central School and had to get special permission to work after school hours. I used to go straight from school every night and work until late. I worked seven nights a week for ten shillings. When I was 14 I left school and worked full time. I loved the work. Even on my day off I went to the pictures. I had a free pass for every cinema in town.

Roker Variety Theatre.

When I was 16 I left the Roker to become second projectionist at the Savoy. It was there that I met my future wife Kitty who worked there as an usherette.

After doing my national service I worked at the Millfield on Hylton Road and then Mrs Tindle asked me to go to the Cora as chief projectionist at 4 guineas a week.

Albert Anderson

SECTION FOUR

SCHOOLDAYS

Church High School ... Colliery School ... Hendon Board ... Jimmy Willies ... St Patrick's ... Redby ...

A class at Stansfield Street School just before the First World War.

Southwick National School

Children's payments for the year ending 30th June 1838 at the Southwick National School amounted to £19 15s 10d, another £44 5s 9d came from subscriptions and donations.

The school's expenditure of £57 4s 11^{1}/$_{2}$d went on:

School Furniture etc – £13 0s 2d
Books, Printing etc – £23 1s 11d
Tea, Brooms, Brushes – £4 9s 6^{1}/$_{2}$d
Mistresses Salary – £16 13s 4d

Rules to be observed by parents of girls attending Southwick National School included:
* Children to be admitted from three years old and upwards, the first Tuesday in every month.
* Two-pence a Week is to be paid in advance, on Monday morning, for every single child; and one penny for every additional child of the same family; if this be neglected, the child will be sent back till it is paid.
* School doors will be open at half-past eight o'clock. School hours are from nine o'clock till twelve at noon; in the afternoon, from half-past one till four o'clock, from the beginning of November till the end of February; and from two till five, from the beginning of March till the end of October.
* The children to come to school with clean hands and faces, their hair cut short and combed, and their clothes neatly mended; if this be neglected, they will be sent home to get it done. No ornaments allowed.

Stone Throwing

In June 1842 eleven-year-old Thomas Stones of Wood Lane was charged with throwing stones at the scholars of the National School, Bishopwearmouth. He was to be fined 5/- if found throwing again or serve 14 days in the House of Correction.

Deptford Yard School

James Laing opened his Deptford Yard School in 1868 for children of his shipyard workers. Children continued to be educated there until Simpson Street School opened in 1884.

The buildings in Toward Road (formerly Park Terrace) as they are today, that originally housed Sunderland Church High School in 1884.

A advertisement for the opening of Sunderland Church High School in 1884. The fees for the year ranged from 9 to 15 guineas a year.

A Commercial Road Girls' School class in the early 1960s. In 1935 the old Commercial Road buildings were remodelled and new ones built. When the scheme was completed the total cost of the work had reached £33,000. The majority of these buildings have now been demolished. What remains today houses Grangetown Primary School.

Mr Floret's class at Barnes Boys' School, *circa* 1958. Keith Summers is centre, second row from front. Other boys include: Charlie Younger, Brian Bailey, Owen Williamson, Billy Burnett, Ian Finlay, Charlie McGregor and the Smith brothers.

The Colliery School

In November 1854 the miners of Monkwearmouth Colliery formed an education society. The men agreed to deductions from their wages to establish a school for their children. A few days before Christmas 1854, 300 children (boys and girls) were being educated at the Colliery School during the day and 100 at the evening school.

Three pence per week was deducted from the wage of each householder working at the colliery to pay for their children's schooling.

The school became overcrowded and on 7th September 1861 a new Colliery School was opened opposite the Wheatsheaf. The new buildings consisted of a boys' room and girls' room of 100ft x 20ft dimension each, an infant school 40ft x 20ft and three classrooms of 20ft x 16ft as well as lavatories and playground.

Wednesday 30th September 1931 was the last time children had lessons at the Colliery School. The following day the 900 scholars moved to the newly built Grange Park School.

The Colliery School buildings today. Builders and Joinery Manufacturers G.M. & G. Marley occupy part of the old school.

A school mural which has survived on a wall of the workshop.

After the last pupils were transferred to Grange Park, the Colliery School was used by the Council's building department. After the war builder George Marley set up business there. Today his son George Jnr runs the workshop (*left*).

The Log Book of the Colliery Boys' School gives an insight into life in the last century up to the First World War.

1st November 1889
An epidemic of measles and fever raged through the school – 84 children were absent and a quarter of the teaching staff. The following week a further dozen pupils went down sick.

7th December 1900
It was reported some boys at the Colliery School had been absent since the summer holidays. The following week three parents of the truant boys were fined five shillings each.

25th April 1902
'There is again a tendency for the children to absent themselves on Friday afternoons, especially on the pay Friday. This afternoon's attendance is the worst experienced for some considerable time.'

20th April 1915
'Arrangements have been made for the boys to attend the Public Swimming Baths each Tuesday morning at 10.15.'

3rd April 1916
'On the evening of April 1st a German Zeppelin visited this town and dropped several bombs within 100 yards of the school. From enquiries this morning none of the children attending here has been injured. Though in many instances the windows of their houses have been shattered to fragments.'

13 July 1916
'School Sports are being held this afternoon. The proceeds are being donated to the scheme for the feeding of poor Belgian children.'

25 January 1918
'During Tank Week the boys bought 81 War Savings Certificates amounting to £62 15s 6d and a £5 War bond.'

A school map made of plaster above the old fireplace. The teacher used to stand by the fire with the children's desks facing. One old pupil who visited the workshop recalled how some children went to school barefoot.

Colliery School Footballers

One of the most famous former pupils of the Colliery School was Fred Thompson. Thompson played in goal for Bury in their 4-0 victory over Southampton in the FA Cup Final. The former Colliery Schoolboy kept a clean sheet in the Final at Crystal Palace on 21st April 1900.

During the First World War two Colliery School lads appeared for England Schoolboys. In 1915 William Charlton played centre forward against Scotland and Wales. The following year full back Richard Hughes had the honour of captaining England against the same countries.

Hendon Board School

The official opening of Hendon Board School took place on 6th January 1879. The school fees were: Boys Department 4d per week; Girls' Department 3d per week; Infants' Department 1d per week. When four members of a family attended the school, the eldest child was taught free and when three of a family attended, the youngest was educated free.

Raich Carter

Hendon Board's most famous pupil was the Sunderland and England footballer Raich Carter. At school Raich excelled at sport. At football he captained England Boys, he was a good cricketer and a fine runner. The day he left school he was presented with a gold medal. The inscription read:

H.S. Carter
From the Pupils and Teachers of
Hendon Boys School, Sunderland.
1927. Cricket, 111 runs in 25 minutes
(in Final).
1928. Football (Captain of English
team), July 1928.

Horatio 'Raich' Carter

Hendon Board Boys' School gymnastic team, *circa* 1950. The PE teacher is Jack Washington who became an emergency trained teacher after the war. Hendon Board was Jack's first appointment in 1947 and he taught there for ten years.

Hendon Board Juniors, *circa* 1949. Matty Morrison is on the left of the front row.

Hendon Board Boys' School teachers in the early 1950s. Standing left to right: Jack Washington, Fred Whiting, Frank Randolf, Bob Storr, Mr Dockray, Walter Hooker, Ron Bell. Sitting: Jim Cowens, Miss Wright, Arnold Rutter, Mr Johnstone, Bill Taylor.

James William Street School was the first elementary school built by Sunderland School Board. The Mayor, A.G. McKenzie performed the opening ceremony on 6th January 1874. The Mayor said: 'There are a large number of people who care nothing about the education of their children, and I hope the Act of Parliament will continue to compel these parents to send their children to school, and they will not be allowed to bring them up so as to fill our gaols and our workhouses and asylums'.

Lucky Girl

The first Mistress of the Girls' Department of James William Street School in 1874 was Sarah Jane Griffiths.

The first girl admitted into the school was presented with a sovereign by the Chairman of the Board.

The 1896 Report of the East End Commissioners gave details of education in the area.

There are 3 Board Schools –

Garden Street,	with 546 in average attendance.
James William Street,	.. 1058	..
The Moor,	.. 585	..
Total	2189

And 3 Voluntary Schools –

The Gray,	with 764 in average attendance.
St John's,	.. 439	..
St Patrick's (RC)	.. 471	..
Total	1674

The boys attended better than girls because girls were frequently kept away to do work at home. Children were found to stay up almost as late as their parents. 'On Saturday nights, quite young children are seen carrying the beer jug, and tasting its contents, till 11 o'clock; and midnight hardly finds them all at home.'

St Patrick's School, *circa* 1957, with the Garths in the background.

St Patrick's School

St Patrick's School opened on 8th May 1871. A week later an entry in the school log book noted: 'Children cautioned against irregular attendance and coming late. Find them much addicted to latter'.

In October 1906 a new St Patrick's School was opened by Father O'Donoghue. The new school's interior walls had glazed bricks to a height of 5 feet with coloured plain brickwork to the ceiling. A total of 570 seniors moved from the old school to the new building. The old school was then used entirely by infants.

Rivals

St Patrick's and James William Street were great rivals on the football field. Games were always fiercely contested and the winners would claim to be the East End's top team – until the next encounter between St Pat's and Jimmy Willies.

Norman Pounder

Right: An advert from the *Sunderland Daily Echo* of 22nd April 1876 announcing the opening of Garden Street School, one of two Board Schools which opened on the same day, the other being Thomas Street, Monkwearmouth. Fees were charged in Sunderland Board Schools until 1891 when elementary education became free.

SUNDERLAND SCHOOL BOARD.—

OPENING OF BOARD SCHOOL.

The New Board Schools in Garden-street will be OPENED on Monday, the 24th April, 1876.

Girls' Mistress .... Miss McCaskell.
Infants' Mistress .... Miss Bruce.

The Fees charged will be as follows :— .

Girls under Seven Years of age .... 2d per week.
  ,, Seven Years of age and upwards .... 3d ,, ,,
Boys under Seven Years of age .... 2d ,, ,,

In cases where three children in one family attend the School, the third child will be admitted Free.

School Hours—Morning .... 9 a.m. to 12
  ,,   ,,   Afternoon .... 1 30 p.m. to 4.
        THOMAS C. McKENZIE,
              Clerk to the School Board.

11th April, 1876.

West Park Central Boys' School, September 1952.

Bishopwearmouth School, 1952. Ted Campbell is second from right, back row and his sister Brenda is second from left, front row. The class also includes: Nancy Knox, Ivy Hunter, Robbie Large, Tony Braid, Mervyn Peacock, Billy Collier, Alfie Stevens, Kenny Stanton, Davy Robson, Wilfy Gray, Kenny Wilkinson, Miriam Burton, John Smith, Davy Lundy, Alan Paterson, Denis White and Wendy Innes. At the front centre are Headmaster Mr Durrant (left) and Mr Chalk.

Footballing Teacher

After the First World War the famous Sunderland and England footballer Charlie Buchan used to teach at Cowan Terrace School. He recalled his time there in his autobiography *A Lifetime in Football*:

During my teaching days, I had lots of opportunities for practice. Each class of the school had one half-day each week free for playing games on a local field. Because some of my fellow teachers were not strong in teaching outdoor sports, I got the job three or four times each week.

Havelock School

Havelock School was the first in town to re-open after the outbreak of the war. Around one thousand children returned to the School's Senior, Junior and Infant departments on Monday 6th November 1939. The decision was made because the school was in a non-evacuation zone and in addition full shelter trenches for children had been completed.

More peaceful times at Havelock Secondary Modern School – An art class in the 1950s.

Havelock Secondary Modern School, *circa* 1954.

Stansfield Street School in 1947. Back row, from the left: Joan Curry, Sheila Roberts, Doreen Ingram, Joan Cruickshanks, Margaret Baines, Margaret Rolfe, Vera Rowntree, Sheila Coulson and Brenda Latimer. Middle row: Ethel Bulmer, Edith Johnson, Jean Stevenson, Olive Conley, Dorothy Masters, Thelma Rigg, Jean Tenent, Joan Teasdale, Norma Young, Jean Crieghton and Emily Waiter. Front row: Elizabeth Stevenson, Madelaine Cronin, Joyce Thompson, Julie Gibson, Joyce Brown, Brenda Lyndsey, Florence Gardiner, Joyce Nicholson and Grace Haddick.

Stansfield Street Teachers

Teachers at Stansfield Street in the 1950s included: Mrs Chapman, Miss Potts, Miss Whaley, Miss War, Miss Mackenzie, Miss Gorley, Miss Gordon (cookery teacher) and Mrs Butterfield (Headmistress)

Left: Mrs Butterfield, Headmistress of Stansfield Street School with students and trophies in the 1950s.

Thomas Street School, *circa* 1952. Headmaster Mr Price is on the right.

Thomas Street Mixed Junior School, 1958. Back row, left to right: Jimmy Patterson, Paul Clark Taylor, Martin Hutchinson, John Jobling, Peter Elliot. Third row: Joe Armstrong, Dennis ?, Alan Quinn, Laurence Falconer, Malcolm Mason, Jimmy Robertson, Bobby Lane. Second row: Eileen Bradley, Susan McCormack, June Martin, Vera Harvey, Joyce Cutter, Violet Simpson, Kathleen Wilson, Margaret Watts. Front row: Jean Sydney, Valerie Patterson, Lillian Robinson, Ann Copus, Elizabeth Thoms, Mary Oxberry, Jean Gowland, Margaret Charters. Standing: Headmaster Mr Price (left) and Mr Turpin (class teacher).

Deptford Terrace

Deptford Terrace closed in the summer of 1961 and was demolished to make way for a glass works. The school's last headmaster Mr E.A. Wilson said 'This school of ours has been a training ground for generations of shipbuilding craftsmen and glass workers. This district has long been famous for glass – before the days of Pyrex and the Hartley Glass Works'. It was fitting, therefore, that the school should go to make way for the glass industry.

Chester Road

When Chester Road School opened in August 1895 the first headmaster of the Boys' Department was J.T. Grayston. Grayston had an earlier claim to fame – he was one of the founders of Sunderland AFC in 1879. The club had been formed by local schoolmasters but dropped the name 'Teachers' from their title early on.

Below: The old Diamond Hall Junior School shortly before its demolition. Work started on the construction of Diamond Hall School in the summer of 1876 and was not completed until the spring of 1878. It was built on a vacant site on the Diamond Hall estate from which it took its name.

Above: A wintry scene of Simpson Street School looking up Wellington Lane. The school had to contend with a 35 feet difference in height from one end to the other. Simpson Street was three times as long as its width and tapered to a point at the west end. Although no longer a school, the building is still in use today, housing factory units.

Carol Summers (centre) on her first day at Pallion School in 1953. The children had their names pinned to their clothes. At this time children still used chalk and little blackboards. In the background is the class playhouse – Pallion Villas.

Valley Road School

Hendon Valley Road School opened on 29th September 1884. Hendon Valley used to be a popular area of recreation with part of the valley laid out as a pleasure garden for the public.

When completed, after a year of building work, the school had room for 420 girls, 480 boys and 414 infants.

Left: The laying of the foundation stone for the new Valley Road Infant School on 20th October 1948. Alderman Harvey, chairman of Sunderland Education Works Sub-committee performed the ceremony.

Below: A Valley Road class in the 1960s. Aubrey Harvey is second from right, second row from the back.

A class at Valley Road School around 1927. Well known local historian Billy Bell is on the right of the front row.

A class from Valley Road over thirty years later. Billy Bell's son David is standing (fifth from left, back row).

Teacher's Long Journey

Mr Brewer, one of the teachers between the wars, lived in South Shields and cycled to and from Valley Road each day.

Billy Bell

Pupils and teachers from St Mary's School at the bottom of Chester Road in 1921. Opened in 1823, the building originally housed an infirmary. In 1831-32 cholera victims were treated there during the epidemic that struck the town. After being used by Primitive Methodists as a training college and chapel it became a Catholic School. In February 1919 there were 375 boys and 363 girls on St Mary's School roll. Today St Mary's is part of the University of Sunderland campus.

Mrs Ritson's class at Barnes Juniors around 1959. Ann Carr is third from right, second row.

Redby School
By Phil Curtis

Queen Victoria was on the throne, Mafeking was under siege, the nineteenth century was coming to a close and it was a cold, windy Friday. Such was the day, 1st December 1899, when Redby opened its doors to children for the very first time.

Famous local dignitaries turned up that day. In attendance were members of the local School Board including Messrs. Abbs, Backhouse (his garden became Backhouse Park), Davison, Bartram and Blumer (shipbuilders) as well as the Headmistress, Miss A. Iley and her staff comprising Lilian Marshall (Deputy), Sarah Davison, Mary Sands and Kate Tracey. Miss Iley had previously been Headmistress at James William Street School (affectionately known in the East End as 'Jimmy Willies'). Sixty three children turned up on that first day and numbers quickly increased throughout the next few months.

Miss Iley, the first Headmistress at Redby.

The first winter was a very bad one but Miss Iley reported that, 'The school is warm and cosy in spite of the intense cold', When snow fell the children, on entering, were obliged to rub their boots with a duster to remove the snow.

The first unscheduled holiday occurred on 21st May 1900 when, after assembling, the school was dismissed for the day to celebrate the 'Relief of Mafeking'.

The school prospered throughout the Edwardian period. Holidays were supplemented with special days off to celebrate the end of the Boer War as well as the Coronation of King Edward VII and Queen Alexandra. A visit to

The May Pole in the yard of Redby School in 1908.

Newcastle by the new King and Queen provided more holiday joy for pupils. Race Wednesday (Derby Day) was also a holiday and continued to be so until the early 1950s.

1910 saw the school with a staff of 12 to teach over 500 pupils. In-service training for staff even then had its part to play with a teacher coming from London for two weeks to give staff lessons in Morris Dancing at their own expense. (Oh to have been a fly on the wall!) The same year saw the commencement of an event which was to re-occur later in the century on a regular basis – melted snow poured in through the school roof.

Perhaps the pupil of the decade was Annie Scrafton. From 1903 to 1914 Annie was never absent nor late. Many ex-pupils will remember the Scrafton family – Their shop was directly across the road from the school on the corner of Duke Street. Today, there is a dentistry on the site. Scrafton's shop became a treasure trove to Redby children. Annie recalled that you could have your pick of sweets throughout the shop for one penny. Annie remembered look-outs being posted at the boys' entrance gates whilst pupils came in for a halfpenny woodbine and a match (senior boys no doubt).

Thursday 22nd June 1911 was Coronation Day for King George V and Queen Mary. Councillor Young, the Mayor of the town visited the school for the celebration. The Union Jack was erected in the school yard and each boy saluted as he passed. A tea followed. By May 1913 Miss Iley logged that the school had admitted 3,217 pupils since its opening.

1914 saw the school hit by contagious disease. Measles, scarlet fever and diphtheria accounted for over fifty absentees. A number of deaths followed from diphtheria. Indeed, by June 1914 diphtheria had reached epidemic proportions in the school. Classrooms and cloakrooms were sprayed by the Health Officer. With the number of deaths increasing, classrooms were closed down and children were sent home. Parents were in a panic and were agitating to have the school closed. Only 55% of the school were attending. Many children were removed by parents to other schools. The end of the summer term 1914 must have proved to be a blessing for pupils, parents and staff.

A Redby class in 1926.

Mrs Willkins' class at Redby Juniors in October 1949.

However, diphtheria was to haunt the pupils of Redby over the next twelve months with many deaths occurring.

The year also saw the commencement of World War One and the staff kept up the war effort by doing munitions work on Saturdays – the Headmaster worked on the land.

In 1918 another epidemic hit the school. This time it was influenza. The school had to be closed from 8th November until 6th January with six pupils dying from the disease. All told a total of $11^1/_2$ weeks were lost through the epidemic. At this time pupils, on reaching 11, transferred either to the Girls' or Boys' Departments of Redby Seniors.

The 1920s saw the use of slates as well as pen and ink. Monitors would mix the ink from powder every morning and fill up the inkwells. Nature Study lessons were often supplemented with a visit to Fulwell Dene to view the fauna and flora. Sports Days, initially held at Spark's Farm Field were transferred to Seaburn Camp.

The disease which featured so prominently throughout the early years of the school, diphtheria, struck again in March 1935. Yet again the school was closed. Eighty cases were reported.

At this time pupils leaving the Junior school usually went either to Bede, Monkwearmouth Central, Redby Senior Boys or Fulwell Girls' School.

The 1940s saw the retirement of the school's two longest serving teachers. On 31st January 1944 Miss E.J. Smith retired. She had joined the school on 8th January 1900 as a first year pupil-teacher and had taught at Redby for 44 years. The same number of years had also been served by Miss Laura Scott, who joined the staff on 1st January 1903 and retired on 30th April 1947. Between them they had served Redby for 88 years, seen the effect of contagious disease on the school, worked with three different Headteachers and experienced two World Wars, Miss Smith also taught during the Boer War.

By the early 1950s the school had a regular pupil roll of approximately 480. In 1953 the Coronation of Queen Elizabeth II was celebrated with a 'treat'. All 484 pupils and their teachers attended the Ritz cinema to see the film, 'A Queen is Crowned'.

The old school buildings which had dominated Fulwell Road throughout the 20th Century were eventually demolished in the 1990s. The Infant and Junior schools amalgamated in a new Redby Primary School which was built nearby. One of the old school towers was erected in the entrance to the new school.

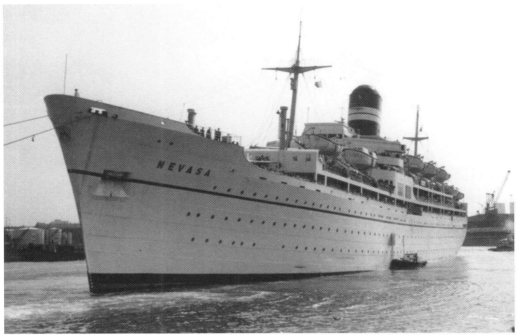

The *Nevasa* leaving Corporation Quay on 20th July 1970 with 1,100 Sunderland schoolchildren on board – bound for Lisbon, the Canary Islands and Casablanca.

The SS *Nevasa* was built in the mid 1950s as a troopship. In the early '60s she was converted to a schoolship.

The *Nevasa* leaving Sunderland Harbour on 20th July 1970. Children had lessons on board but in between there was plenty of entertainment: water polo, hockey, cricket, tug-of-war, quoits and crab football (hands and one foot on the ground at all times).

Pupils from St Joseph's School enjoy a break on deck. Left to right: Stephen Donahue, Micky Smurthwaite, Veronica Wilson, Linda Egan, John Dalzell (standing), Alex Sinclair, Derek Usher, Derek Winlow. Pat Jones (lying on deck).

Linda Egan (right) and Susan Gibson on Mount Teide in Tenerife. The cost of the trip was £60, which was a lot of money in 1970.

Upper VI of Bede Boys Collegiate School in July 1923 while the Oxford School Certificate Examinations were in progress. The Higher Grade School for Sunderland opened on 28th April 1890. The School on West Park later changed its name to the Bede Collegiate School.

In 1929 Bede School moved to new buildings on Durham Road. The 'Bede Centre' now forms part of the City of Sunderland College.

Higher Grade School in the Nineteenth Century

When the Higher Grade School opened in 1890 fees were:

One shilling per week or 10 shillings per quarter, payable in advance. On condition that candidates passed Standard III of the Code.

There were separate schools for Boys and Girls.

Some of the subjects taught in the early years included:

English – Reading, Writing, Recitation, Composition, English Grammar and Analysis.

Mathematics – Arithmetic, Algebra and Euclid.

Languages – French and Latin for Boys, French for Girls.

Girls were also taught Needlework.

A class from Bede Grammar School for Boys in the early 1960s. At this time A.J.B. Budge was headmaster.

Bede football team, March 1970.

Southmoor Technical School

When Southmoor Secondary Technical School for Boys was officially opened by the Mayor on 3rd November 1959 it was hailed as a landmark in Sunderland education. The 1944 Education Act had introduced the Grammar, Secondary and Technical school system. In terms of new building programmes Technical schools came last in priority in funding. Southmoor was seen as showing the town's commitment to fulfilling the Act.

Built at a cost of a quarter of a million pounds, Southmoor replaced the old Junior Technical School in Villiers Street.

Left: Geoff Pearson ready for Southmoor in 1963, with sister Liz. In that year Liz left Broadway Secondary Modern.

A Hylton Castle Juniors class in 1958.

St Thomas Aquinas Girls' School in 1964.

First year Technical Drawing class in 1964 at St Thomas Aquinas Boys' School.
Mr Davies is the teacher.

Five-year-olds at Springwell Infants School in 1951.

St Joseph's, Millfield in July 1972.

Bexhill Junior and Infant Schools

Predicting the Future

One of our teachers at Thomas Street School in the 1950s was Mr Turpin. He once said to our class 'When you get older there will be no shipyards, no work, just leisure time'. All the lads in the class cheered.

Margaret Thynne

Above: A booklet produced for the opening of Bexhill Junior and Infant School on 7th October 1965. The school, with its futuristic hall, was built and fitted out at a cost of £122,000. The opening ceremony was performed by Anthony Crosland MP, Secretary of State for Education and Science.

VICTORIA HALL
DISASTER

*Tragic Saturday Afternoon … Sad Aftermath … The London
Illustrated News … A Survivor's Story … Message From America
… The Last Victim …*

The Victoria Hall with the monument erected to victims of the tragedy in the
foreground.

On 16th June 1883 a tragedy took place in Sunderland that shocked the world. On that fateful Saturday afternoon the Victoria Hall in Toward Road was packed with two thousand children – some as young as 3 years old. They had gone to see the entertainer Alexander Fay with the added inducement of the chance to receive free toys. In the days before the show Fay had gone around the town's schools distributing tickets and handbills.

Near the end of the show children from the gallery rushed down the stairs fearing they would miss out on the free gifts. One of Fay's assistants was trying to control the flow of the children at the bottom of the staircase by keeping the door (which only opened inwards) partly open. The children continued to pile down the staircase until there was a sprawling mass. The few adults present frantically tried to free the pile of small bodies. Although as many as two hundred children were disentangled and saved, 183 children from all parts of Sunderland lost their lives.

As news spread of the disaster people rushed to the scene looking for their loved ones. *A Narrative of the Accident* published in August 1883 recalled one pathetic incident: 'Shortly after the disaster, a little girl, quite a child in appearance, was met proceeding along Tatham Street carrying a dead infant in her arms. A gentleman who witnessed the melancholy sight took compassion on the girl, and at once secured a cab and sent her home in it'.

The well known Sunderland architect Frank Caws spoke to one of the young survivors: 'I asked a baby boy, just able to talk, and who had escaped after being somewhat crushed, "Did you hear the children calling out?" The child said, "Yes". I asked, "What did you hear them say?" "They were calling for their ma's", he replied'.

The following two pages show how the Victoria Hall Disaster made the front page of both *The Illustrated London News* and *The Graphic* a week later.

A view of the Victoria Hall at the turn of the century with children playing in the park.

THE ILLUSTRATED LONDON NEWS.

No. 2305.—VOL. LXXXII.   SATURDAY, JUNE 23, 1883.   WITH TWO SUPPLEMENTS   SIXPENCE. By Post, 6½d.

STAGE OF VICTORIA HALL, FROM THE GALLERY.

DOORWAY, SHOWING THE DOOR WIDE OPEN.

EXTERIOR OF VICTORIA HALL.

TOP OF THE STAIRS LEADING TO THE DOORWAY.

STAIRCASE AND DOORWAY WHERE THE CATASTROPHE HAPPENED.

THE TERRIBLE DISASTER AT SUNDERLAND: TWO HUNDRED CHILDREN CRUSHED TO DEATH.—See Page 635.

THE GRAPHIC

AN ILLUSTRATED WEEKLY NEWSPAPER

No. 708.—VOL. XXVII.
Regd. at General Post Office as a Newspaper

SATURDAY, JUNE 23, 1883

WITH EXTRA SUPPLEMENT

PRICE SIXPENCE
Or by Post Sixpence Halfpenny

1. Exterior View of the Victoria Hall.—2. External Door of the Hall.—3. The Portion of the Staircase Where the Disaster Occurred, Showing the Partly Open Door Which Caused the Accident (The Dotted Line Shows the Height to Which the Children's Bodies Were Heaped Behind the Door and on the Staircase).—4. Another View of the Scene of the Disaster, Showing the Short Flight of Sixteen Steps Leading to the Fatal Door.

THE INTERIOR OF THE VICTORIA HALL

THE TERRIBLE DISASTER AT SUNDERLAND

A Survivor's Story

Ten years after the disaster, Sidney Duncan, the editor and proprietor of the local newspaper *The Blizzard* recalled his lucky escape:

Nothing will remain more indelibly imprinted upon my mind than the memory of the Victoria Hall disaster, out of which I escaped by the merest chance. I was only about ten years of age at the time, and on that never-to-be-forgotten Saturday afternoon was enjoying a game amongst five of my playmates, when a man came forward and presented each of us with a small yellow bill, which, he remarked, would admit us at half-price to the grand entertainment in the Victoria Hall, and entitle us to receive 'a prize gift' at the close of the performance. What remained of our weekly pocket money was soon gathered up; the game was abandoned, and away we rushed to the Hall. Of that half dozen I was the only one who left the building alive. We arrived fully half-an-hour before the commencement of the show, but even the

Childrens Memorial, Mobray Park, Sunderland.

gallery was packed to its utmost capacity with boys and girls. It was a stifling June afternoon, but no heed was paid to the oppressive atmosphere by the youngsters, whose whole attention was soon absorbed in the entertainment. Towards the close, however, 'the prizes' became the general topic of conversation, and, when at last the performance closed, there was a general stampede for the door. I joined in the rush, but after mounting the third seat, turned again, and looked over the gallery rail into the body of the hall. Often since, I have wondered what prompted me to halt. Certainly, I was as eager as any to secure a prize, and after the momentary glance over the rail, I again darted off and commenced to force through to the front of the crowd. This was a comparatively easy task as far as the first flight of stairs was concerned, but on the second I was brought to a full stop. Only a few yards away was the fatal door, and piled up level almost with the landing, were the hapless little ones. Ignorant of the awful catastrophe in front, and anxious only to secure their presents, the children behind still pressed on. Within half a minute I was forced off my feet, and almost buried in the struggling, dying mass. Only the cries of a few who were being crushed in the pack behind, could be heard. In front comparative silence reigned, but the writhings of the expiring little ones were fearful to behold. I witnessed all, and lay unable even to aid myself. Fully five minutes elapsed before assistance arrived. Then the box door on the landing above was opened, several men rushed in, and the work of rescue commenced. When the pressure from behind eased up I soon released myself, and hurried out into the fresh air, into which the dead and dying were soon being carried by dozens of willing workers. Side by side they were laid along the flags; some to recover; others never to open their eyes again. Standing on the steps of the Toward Road entrance I waited for my companions. One after the other they were carried out – dead; they had been in the very fore-front of the rush.

Sidney Duncan
The Blizzard, 8th July 1893

Message From America

A week after the Victoria Hall disaster a leading American newspaper showed the effect the tragedy had overseas.

No woman-heart in all the earth but bleeds for you,
        Mothers of the North!
And strong men groan in sorrow for your loss.
Yet hearten up! Your loss is but for time,
Eternity shall give your darlings back to you.
And 'mid your raining tears take this one thought to heart,—
Your little ones have all got safely home,
And all have won their prizes.

Detroit Free Press
23rd June 1883

Queen Victoria

Queen Victoria, who was the mother of nine children herself, was deeply shocked by the Victoria Hall calamity. She sent a wreath of white flowers with a card inscribed:

A mark of deep sympathy from Queen Victoria. 'Suffer little children come unto me, for of such is the kingdom of Heaven'.

The Last Victim

William Robinson, son of Mr Robinson of the Argo Frigate public house in Bedford Square died on the Wednesday after the tragedy. The 39-year-old, Sunderland Volunteer Life Brigade member, had helped in carrying the bodies out of the Hall. He was never the same after the shock of what he experienced that day. On the Tuesday (three days after the tragedy) he took ill and he died at midnight of the following day.

A Century Later

A few years ago I did a lot of research on the Victoria Hall disaster but I had to stop because it was so sad. Even a century after the tragedy reading about how so many children lost their lives had a great affect on me.

Albert Anderson

The monument to the little victims at present in Bishopwearmouth Cemetery. It bears the inscription:

ERECTED
TO COMMEMORATE
THE CALAMITY WHICH TOOK PLACE
IN THE VICTORIA HALL, SUNDERLAND
ON SATURDAY 16th JUNE 1883
BY WHICH 183 CHILDREN LOST THEIR LIVES

Lucky To Be Alive

When Mrs Emma Monarch celebrated her 100th birthday on 29th April 1975 she knew how lucky she had been to reach the milestone. Born in Woodbine Street, Hendon, one of a family of ten, Emma should have been at the Victoria Hall on the day of the disaster in 1883. Three of her friends called on her to go to the Hall on that fateful day. However, her mother had a feeling that something was going to happen and would not allow her 8-year-old daughter to go. Emma later found out that all three of her friends had died in the crush.

SECTION SIX

WARTIME

Battle Of Jutland ... Peace Medals ... Evacuees ... City Of Benares ... Rations ... Air Raids ...

Certificates like this one were presented to Sunderland schoolchildren who played their part during the two World Wars by sending gifts to servicemen who were stationed overseas.

Above: St Mary Magdalene Church Lads' Brigade, *circa* 1917.

Left: More young lads from the church in Rutland Street, Millfield, this time in uniform.

Below: A performance of 'Flags of the Nations' in February 1917 at St Mary Magdalene Church.

Church Lads' Brigade Cadets at West Park during the First World War.

Battle of Jutland

'My boys i.e. Standard 7 – are drawing a map of part of the North Sea showing where the great naval battle (between the Germans and the English) took place.

Our Grand Fleet came in touch with the German High Seas Fleet at 3.30 on the afternoon of May 31st.

The losses on both sides were severe but when the main body of the British Fleet came into contact with the German High Seas Fleet they were not long before they sought protection in their harbours.

I am afraid many of our old boys, and the fathers of present scholars are among the missing.'

Robinson Street School log book, 5th June 1916

Peace Celebrations

The Peace Celebrations procession set off from West Park on the morning of 19th July 1919. The floats travelled along Toward Road and Borough Road to the East End then back up through the town centre and across the bridge down Roker Avenue to Millum Terrace and Dock Street. The procession then made its way back over the town and up Hylton Road along St Mark's Road down Chester Road and finishing at Cowan Terrace.

The *Sunderland Daily Echo* reported how children were enjoying the day:

A favourite method of disguise was for the boys to dress up as girls and the girls to don boys' clothing. 'The bairns are enjoying themselves, anyway,' remarked one woman to another. 'Aye, aa's sure they are,' replied the second woman; 'let them gan on, poor bairns.' This was part of the spirit of the day, to enjoy and let others enjoy. The masquerading idea was adopted by a great many grown up girls, principally East Enders, who thought it fine fun to go about dressed up as soldiers and sailors.

The 1919 Peace Celebration passes the Derby Hotel in Millum Terrace. Riding alongside children on the float is Wallace the Lion from Sunderland Museum.

Right: A Peace Medal given to Sunderland schoolchildren in 1919. In the year following the end of the First World War many of the town's teachers had returned to their schools after serving in the forces. Nine teachers lost their lives in the conflict: Douglas Tweddie (Redby), Walter R. Goodrick (James William Street), Arthur Coleman (St Joseph's), J.A. Pinchen (Cowan Terrace), Fawcitt Wayman (Valley Road), Cecil Hands (Pallion), Charles L. Patterson (Pallion), Robert H. Stafford (Simpson Street) and James T. Robson (Stansfield Street).

Boys being presented with the Peace Medal at High Barnes School in 1919.

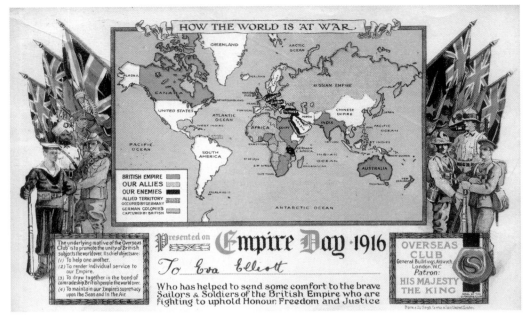

A Certificate awarded to Eva Elliott for contributing towards gifts for overseas servicemen.

The Empire Day Movement was founded in 1903 by the Earl of Meath to instil patriotism into the nation's children. He managed to persuade education authorities to celebrate the anniversary of Queen Victoria's birth. By 1907 more than half the elementary schools in England and Wales were celebrating 24th May – Empire Day.

Last Days of Empire

As late as 1960 we celebrated Empire Day at Commercial Road School. By then I think it might have been known as Commonwealth Day. We were given small Union Jacks to wave in the Assembly Hall. Even at the age of five I knew these flags from the school stores were very old. They must have been taken out of storage for events like Empire Day or Coronations.

Jackie Turnbull

Pupils celebrating Empire Day at Pallion School in the mid '50s.

Redby School in the Wars
By Phil Curtis

During World War One soldiers were billeted in Redby School buildings for a short period. Whilst this took place pupils had to attend Thomas Street School. Redby was opened for business again in May 1916. The move back from Thomas Street proved wise. The night of 1st April 1916 saw an air-raid by the Germans and a bomb and two incendiaries hit Thomas Street School. During this time Redby pupils attended only on mornings with Stansfield Street pupils also using the school premises on the afternoon.

Even though World War Two did not begin until September 1939, the Government issued gas masks to all Redby pupils a year earlier. The war eventually cast its shadow on the school and on 11th September 1939, 175 boys and girls were evacuated to Driffield under the guidance of Mr Prince and five teachers. It was at Driffield in March of the following year that Mr Prince died. He had been with the school for eight years.

Meanwhile, back at the school, air-raid shelters had been arranged in the school grounds and many children returned to the town by April 1940 when the school re-opened. On 1st May 1940 a new Headteacher, Mr C.G. Benson took charge.

The first air-raid warning came on 3rd July 1940 at 1.57 pm. It was recorded that all the children were in shelters within two minutes. With the bombing came more evacuation and many children were then sent to the Bedale area accompanied by Mr Mountford and Miss E.L. Carr. Still the school continued although during 1941 the air-raid siren was to be heard many times but always the pupils quickly retired to the school shelters.

On the evening of 7th March 1941, the school was damaged by enemy bombs. The month of May in that same year again saw the school damaged. On 5th May the school was closed whilst repairs took place and again on 6th May repairs were required. Nearby Duke Street and Francis Street were badly hit with Scrafton's shop suffering damage. The caretaker's house which then stood in the school grounds was badly damaged and had to be demolished. During the early years of the war part of the building was used as an ambulance depot under the leadership of Mr Brown. A stone wall was erected in front of the Secretary's room to prevent bomb damage. During this time the ambulances were stationed in the front yard whilst some of the classrooms were used for stores.

In April 1943 the Mayor of Sunderland, Mr Myers Wayman, visited the school to encourage children to subscribe to the 'Wings for Victory' campaign. By May the school had subscribed £1,355 through its National Savings scheme.

The war years had seen the death of a Headteacher and the retirement of a number of the staff. However, a number of teachers returned to the school including Mr R. Etherington after five years war service.

Scrafton's Shop

In the last war soldiers stayed at Redby School. One day a horse drawn gun carriage was leaving the school when one of the horses went wild. The carriage smashed through the gates and I thought it was going to come into our shop. In May 1941 a bomb landed on our shop and killed my mother Emily Jane. The shop was rebuilt and we continued to serve Redby pupils for many years.

Annie Scrafton

Two days before war was declared on 3rd September 1939, Britain set in motion the task of evacuating three million mothers, children and disabled from the towns and cities. Sunderland's evacuation plan was delayed and it was not until the 10th September that the first trains carrying evacuees left for the countryside.

Right: Mothers and under school age children outside the Jeffrey Hall, Monk Street (Wheatsheaf) before they were evacuated to Driffield, Yorkshire at the start of the war. Back row, left to right: Mrs Elsie Young, Mrs French, Mrs Katie Spours holding her son Edwin aged 9 months, Mrs Curtis holding her daughter Brenda. Front row: Brenda Spours aged 3, Norman French aged 3, Pat Curtis aged 3 and Freddy Young aged 3. Most of these were back home again by Christmas 1939.

Further evacuation schemes followed – Youngsters line up in Hudson Road School Yard in the summer of 1940. On 7th and 8th July, 1,761 children left by train from Millfield and Monkwearmouth stations for the Yorkshire countryside. Along with their small bundles of personal possessions, sandwiches and gas masks, the children have labels with their name around their necks or pinned to clothing.

The Loss of the *City of Benares*

One of the saddest incidents of the last war involving Sunderland children was the sinking of the SS *City of Benares*. The Government set up a scheme to evacuate children overseas in 1940. One of the ships carrying children under the scheme was the *City of Benares* which left Liverpool on Friday 13th September 1940 bound for Canada. Among the 90 children on board were eleven from Sunderland.

Four days into the voyage the children's ship was sunk by a torpedo from a German U-boat. The attack came at night when the children were asleep in their bunks. Even those who made it to the lifeboats had to endure days at sea in freezing weather. Seventy seven children perished in the icy waters of the Atlantic. Eleanor Wright and Billy Short were the only survivors from the Sunderland party. Billy Short's five-year-old brother Peter was one of

Survivors from the City of Benares Eleanor Wright (aged 13) and Billy Short (aged 9) on their return to Sunderland. Billy had been reported as one of those who had been lost.

those who did not make it. As she was recovering from her ordeal in hospital Eleanor told of the heroism of one of the Sunderland boys who died. 'George Crawford was a hero. When the boats had been launched in the rough seas a little boy from London named Walder fell into the water. George leaned over the side and caught hold of him. After he had dragged him to safety he lost his balance and fell into the sea. I saw him no more.'

The other Sunderland children who died in the tragedy were: sisters Edith (aged 13) and Irene (aged 11) Smith, brother and sister Thomas (aged 9) and Anne (aged 6) Watson, George Crawford (aged 14), Maureen Dixon (aged 10), Derek Leigh (aged 11) and Dorothy Wood (aged 9).

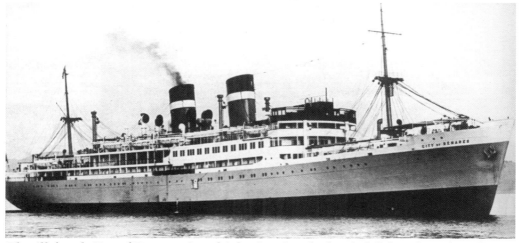

The ill-fated *City of Benares* in which nine Sunderland children lost their lives.

Sweet Potatoes

In 1941 a Kitchen Front and Dig for Victory Week was held in Sunderland. Demonstrations in wartime cookery were given in the town's schools. A booklet of recipes was also published. Included in this was a section on cakes and biscuits for children. As well as instructions on how to make digestive biscuits, oatmeal cookies and wholemeal cakes there was a recipe for chocolate potato cake.

Chocolate Potato Cake

2ozs. Fat. 2ozs. Sugar, 1 tablesp. Dry Mashed Potato, 2 tablesp. Flour, 1 level teasp. Baking Powder, 1 good teasp. Cocoa, $^1/_4$ cup Milk, A few drops Vanilla Essence.

Beat the margarine and sugar together. Add the vanilla essence, cocoa and a little milk, add all other dry ingredients with the rest of the milk in 3 or 4 portions. Stir well. Lastly, mix in the potatoes. Put in greased bun tins and bake in a fairly hot oven for 10-15 minutes.

Clara Carrot

The spice of life is very much Clara Carrot's concern; for she's a master of variety — a quick - change artist with a hundred and one disguises, each more amusing than the last. If you've only met her plain and boiled you've no idea how delightful she can be in other modes. You should try

Jugged Brisket

Various campaigns were run during the war to get people to eat certain foodstuffs. This Walt Disney cartoon from the *Sunderland Echo* of 1941 encouraged local children to eat vegetables.

The *Echo*, Christmas 1941, advertising a brand of sweets which is still going strong today.

Sweet Rationing

To the disappointment of the nation's children sweet rationing was introduced in July 1942 (2 ounces per week). Even when the war ended sweets continued to be rationed. They were eventually de-rationed on Sunday 24th April 1949 but this was to prove short-lived. When local shopkeepers went to open up on the Monday they found long queues awaiting them. In one Sunderland shop a woman bought 50 bars of chocolate while others were buying five, ten or 15 shillings worth of sweets.

Similar scenes were witnessed all round the country and the Government had no option but to reintroduce sweet rationing, which they did on 14th August 1949. This in turn led to long queues of children waiting for sweetshops to open on the first day after the return of rationing. By mid-day one local sweetshop had served 2,014 customers, around two thirds of whom were children. The favourite item sought after were lollipops.

When sweets finally came off the ration for good on 4th February 1953 most shops were able to cope with demand. However, on the evening of the announcement one shop in Sunderland put a 'Sweets Off Ration!' notice on their window but by the next morning they had sold out.

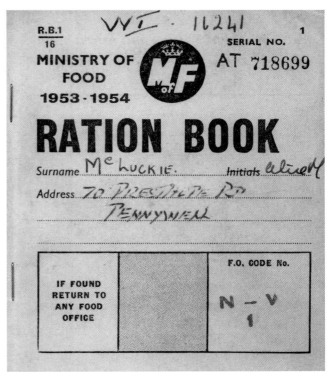

A Sunderland resident's post-war Ration Book – for children the most important page was the Sweets Points

Made In Germany

A letter to the Editor of the *Sunderland Echo* of 4th December 1940 revealed a less than patriotic Christmas toy on sale in Sunderland.

Sir,— A friend of mine purchased a doll in Sunderland, the price being 13s 6d for an article retailing at about 7s pre-war. Imagine her surprise on examining it at home to find the mark "Made in Germany" clearly exhibited.

Obviously it is pre-war stock. Now who is profiteering? No doubt the retailer will blame the wholesaler and the wholesaler the importers, etc, etc.

It is bad enough to be "paying through the nose" without having the "Made in Germany" labels thrust at us on our children's toys.

H.P.

Presents From Home

Before breaking up for their holidays in December 1940, West Park Central School sent off Christmas gifts to former pupils serving in the Forces. One hundred and fifty packages were dispatched. Men received: a book, shaving soap, razor blades, sweets, cigarettes, woollen comfort and a handkerchief. Cold Cream and toilet soap replaced shaving soap and razor blades in the women's parcels.

Priority Case

Near the end of the last war, when I was only about 3 years old, I remember being sent to the butcher's on a message for my mother. The shop on the corner of Tatham Street and Ward Street was owned by Mr Richardson.

At this time my dad was away in the Forces and my mam was expecting. I went straight to the front of the queue and when one customer complained Mr Richardson said this boy has priority. Everytime I went in the shop I was served straight away. This happened right up to the late '60s when the shop was demolished!

Matty Morrison

This photograph was taken in the backyard of 16 Mulgrave Street, Monkwearmouth. The year was 1947. On my knee is my sister Muriel and left of me is my friend Betty and her brother Harry. We all lived in the same building.

Behind us is an air-raid shelter, one of many to be built in the area. The inside was made very comfortable with cushions on the bunks (as we called them), an old clippie mat that covered the stone floor and a curtain that hung from the entrance. As we weren't allowed to go far during the war years, we would spend many an hour playing in the shelter which made our mams feel at ease knowing where we were. Shortly after this photo was taken it was demolished and for us children it was a very sad day indeed.

Joan Quinn

Children playing in newly dug Air Raid Precaution (ARP) trenches on Sunderland Town Moor in October 1938. St John's Church can be seen in the background.

Air-Raids

During air-raids in the last war we used to go into a shelter in Tavistock Place. On one occasion we did not make it to the shelter before the bombs started dropping. A large plate glass window came in on us. A piece of flying glass hit my four-year-old daughter Lily in the head. We rushed her to the First Aid Centre. She needed stitches in the top of her head and still has the scar to this day.

Everyone was terrified during the air-raids. It was thought gas would be dropped and everyone (including children) had to carry gas masks everywhere with them.

Lily Turnbull

Left: A milkman making a delivery at the end of Duke Street, Roker in 1930. This house was destroyed in an air-raid during the war.

Norma Johnson in her pram outside 47 Dock Street in the late 1930s. Bradbury the Undertakers is opposite. Railings like those in the picture were a valuable source of metal for the war effort.

Two young girls ready to leave Sunderland Station in May 1944, after visiting relations in the town.

Spitfire Fund

Children played their part in the war effort by raising money for causes like the Spitfire Fund. A heavy raid by the Luftwaffe in the summer of 1940 gave the Fund a boost. The *Sunderland Echo* of 19th August reported how thousands of Sunderland people visited districts damaged in an air raid the previous week: 'Outside one house, damaged when a bomb burst at the front of the garden, stood the small daughter of the occupant. She rattled a collecting box and displayed a neatly-printed notice "We don't want any more of this – help us to buy that Spitfire." '

The article went on to report how money was pouring in to the Treasurer's Office in Sunderland Town Hall from children wanting to help the Spitfire Fund.

'Lena Coates, John Errington, Irene Ord, Marjorie Newham, Margaret Jackman, Barbara Truman, Harry Jackman and Brian Jackman, held two concerts in a backyard in Sydenham Terrace and raised £2 10s 6d for the Mayor's Spitfire Fund.

'A jumble sale held by the children of Beverley Road, Grangetown, has raised £3 10s for the Spitfire Fund.

'Rose Douglas, Marion Cousins, Irene Robson, Matilda Hindson, and Eileen Gardner organized a jumble sale in aid of the Fund in Hood Street on Saturday, and obtained £1 13s 9d.

'Six Southwick girls, Winnie Khalbom, Winnie Brunton, Iris and Jean McGill and Joan and Audrey Kelly, raised £1 11s 3d for the Fund with a jumble sale on Saturday.'

POOR BAIRNS

Feeding The Poor Bairns ... Begging ... Cruelty ... The Workhouse ... Barefoot In Winter ... Cottage Homes Nightmare ...

Youngsters on the quayside in the last century.

Feeding the Poor Bairns

Over the years children have been severely affected by poverty when their parents have been unemployed or off work through sickness. In the nineteenth and twentieth century Sunderland suffered seasonal unemployment in the shipyards. For example output from the town's yards fell from 200,000 tons in 1883 to 61,771 in 1885. In 1908 half the labour force in the shipyards were unemployed.

Children were often victims of these economic trends and sometimes paid the ultimate price for their parents' unemployment. On 6th August 1842 Caroline Fortune the infant daughter of an unemployed joiner living in Pemberton Buildings, Bishopwearmouth died of starvation. At the inquest held the following month the child's mother Mary Fortune gave evidence: 'On Monday, the 1st of August, I went to Mr Hutchinson (Relieving Officer) and received one shilling; I told him that we had not eaten anything for two days, except some cold potatoes some of the neighbours had given us'.

The inquest jury returned a verdict that the child had died from starvation and cast severe censure on Mr Hutchinson for being 'culpable and inhumane'.

In December 1878 soup kitchens were set up in the West End of Sunderland. Demand quickly grew:

Thursday 5th	90 gallons of soup, 17½ stones of bread
Saturday 7th	150 gallons of soup, 36½ stones of bread
Tuesday 10th	200 gallons of soup, 56½ stones of bread

A lot of the money to pay for the soup kitchens came from the town's workforce. Men at Pallion Engine Works subscribed 2d a week and boys a penny, Corporation cartmen and sawmill workers in the Docks were just a few who helped feed Sunderland's poor at this time.

> REOPENING OF THE
> **BOROUGH SOUP KITCHENS.**
> A PUBLIC MEETING
> WILL BE HELD
> IN THE POLICE COURT, EAST CROSS STREET, SUNDERLAND,
> ON TUESDAY NEXT, NOVEMBER 30TH,
> AT TWELVE O'CLOCK AT NOON,
>
> TO take into consideration the necessity of immediately RE-OPENING the SOUP KITCHENS of the Borough, to alleviate the distress at present so largely prevailing.
> THE MAYOR WILL PRESIDE.
> The Attendance of all Classes is Invited.

Above: A public meeting to discuss the re-opening of the Borough Soup Kitchen advertised in the *Sunderland Herald* of 26th November 1858.

Hungry Children

During the 1830s and '40s many children were caught stealing food.

On 26th October 1840 seven boys aged between 8 and 12 from Monkwearmouth Shore were charged with stealing beans and corn from Bent House Farm near Whitburn. The boys were reprimanded and discharged.

The fields belonging to landowner Sir Hedworth Williamson at Monkwearmouth were often the target of raids. On 18th October 1841 Thomas Ewings (aged 12), John Ewings (aged 10), John Maxwell (aged 12) and John Rose (aged 12) were fined for stealing turnips from a field belonging to Williamson near the North Dock. Nine days later a girl and two boys were caught stealing potatoes from another Williamson field. A week later another raiding party was caught: William Eiley (aged 13), Margaret Eiley (aged 11), Eleanor Muckel (aged 10), Alice Muckel (aged 8), Elizabeth Peacock (aged 10) and Henry Tate (aged 12). All were local children and were discharged promising not to offend again.

Soup Kitchens

In his book *Back on the Borough Beat*, John Yearnshire described how Police in Sunderland helped alleviate hunger in poor areas of town during the 1920s:

'Two men from each Division called at fruiterers and collected carrots, turnips, peas and cabbage. Likewise, at pork and butchers shops, bone, fat and meat were obtained. Six boilers were erected in the Fire Station yard manned by policemen who had experience of field cooking during the war. The soup that was made was then carried in urns from Gill Bridge Avenue to the issuing points for distribution to those in need.'

Children at a soup kitchen in Sunderland manned by Inspector Wilkinson and his colleagues.

Feeding the Bairns

In April 1884 at a meeting of the Distress Committee in John Street it was reported that 400 children in the East End and Hendon were receiving breakfasts. In Monkwearmouth poor children were given breakfast one day and a dinner the next. At 12.30 pm on 28th April 1884 a group of 300 children assembled at Millum Terrace Coffee Tavern for a meal. This consisted of pea-soup and three slices of bread for each child. The *Sunderland Daily Echo* the following day reported, 'Before these breakfasts began, they say, a good many of the children had been living from day to day on a meal of potatoes; and on the first occasion that a breakfast was given the little ones could not repress tears of gratitude'.

Stigma

I remember the first day of a new school year at Commercial Road in the early '60s. I was around eight years old at the time. The woman teacher asked for those in class who would be staying for free dinners to put up their hand. I knew I had to have them but I was too embarrassed to raise my hand. When I turned up at home at dinner time my mam went mad. She went down to school and told them off for showing up the less well off kids.

Tommy Taylor

Begging on the Streets

In the 1830s and '40s many children were charged with begging on the streets of Sunderland.

Ann Donnolly was nine years old when she was found begging in an apparent state of destitution in Church Street in December 1838.

A few weeks later Margaret Langas (aged 7) from Ireland was found begging in the Arcade. She was discharged on condition she promised to leave town. This was the means by which the authorities rid themselves of the problem of beggars from outside of town. On 6th July 1842 three Irish girls, Margaret Hassan (aged 10), Elizabeth Fox (aged 8) and Catherine Gooley (aged 8) were charged with begging in the Parish of Bishopwearmouth. The charges were to be dropped if they left town but if found again they were to be committed.

FORM XX.)

National Society for the Prevention of Cruelty to Children.

PATRON - THE QUEEN.

SUNDERLAND & DISTRICT BRANCH.

In Cases of Cruelty what to do.

Act of Parliament 57 & 58 Victoria, Chap. 41.

Persons knowing of **Assault, Ill-treatment, Neglect, Abandonment,** or **Exposure** of any children **in a manner likely to cause them unnecessary suffering or injury to their health,** should communicate immediately with the Local Hon. Secretary :

Mr. H. SALISBURY SQUANCE,

LOCAL OFFICE—

7, New Durham Road,

SUNDERLAND.

• All further steps will be taken, and expenses borne, by the Society.

Names of Informants will be kept strictly private.

[P.T.O.

A Sunderland Branch NSPCC leaflet from 1894.

Little Twinkle

Ten-year-old Sarah Twinkle was charged with destitution in High Street, Bishopwearmouth on 1st June 1840. She was discharged on condition she went back to her aunt.

Corporal Punishment

When ten-year-old Robert Forbes of High Street appeared in court for stealing 3/6d from a lady in February 1842 – his sentence was 'to have a whipping'.

NSPCC

A meeting of the Sunderland Branch of the National Society for the Prevention of Cruelty to Children was held on 24th March 1922. With the Mayor Councillor Raine in the chair, the meeting were, 'encouraged to find the worst forms of cruelty to children was occurring less frequently.' However, there were still 181 cases in Sunderland and District dealt with in the previous year. These affected 582 children and 222 offenders, five of whom were prosecuted (all convicted).

Workhouse Life

In 1797 a Report on *The State of the Poor* was produced by Sir F.M. Eden which included evidence gathered in Sunderland:

'The Poor are supported partly in a Workhouse, partly at home. There are 176 persons at present in the house. There are 36 children ... who are employed in a pin factory. The boys are generally bound apprentices to the sea service. '

The Report went on to describe the Workhouse diet:

Breakfast	Every day – Hasty pudding* and milk
Dinner	Sunday, Thursday – Beef and bread
	Monday, Friday – Old milk and bread
	Tuesday – Pease soup and bread
	Wednesday – Rice-milk and bread
	Saturday – Barley-milk and bread
Supper	Sunday, Thursday – bread and broth
	Monday, Friday – Water gruel and bread
	Tuesday – Boiled milk and bread
	Wednesday, Saturday – Boiled milk or gruel and bread

* flour stirred to thick batter in boiling milk or water

The bread is made of wheat and rye. 6 oz are allowed to each person at dinner and supper on meat days, and on other days, $^1/_2$lb at each meal; $^1/_2$lb meat is served to each person on Sunday and Thursday. The victuals cost about £26 a week.

The New Workhouse in Chester Road

The *Sunderland Echo* of 3rd January 1974 printed a letter from a Wearside exile recalling the hard days of his childhood early in the century:

The poverty one can never erase from one's memory but the remembrance of heroic parents who did so much to make life bearable in the home, does help to counterbalance the shame of poverty. I have seen poverty in other places and it has reduced many to a pathetic disillusioned state, but somehow at home I believe the town's motto, Nil desperandum, ran through the hearts of many like a golden thread.

I think of the Jolly Jumbles at the foot of Holey Rock, the pierrot show now forgotten, the Workhouse picnic, when the annual fair gave all the inhabitants of Highfield* free goes on all the sideshows and roundabouts, public admission $^1/_2$d. The thrill of the greasy pole with its little red purses hanging from the cross piece, and the excitement of seeing the hot air balloon leave the ground.

The Town Moor, with its annual fair, and the houses in the vicinity all decorated and awarded prizes. These were our holiday treats, and I can remember the thrill on getting a ticket from Pearson's Fresh Air Fund which transported us to Seaham and Dawdon Dene ...

I call to mind many of the characters that Sunderland held, Sally the fish wife, with her marvellous sense of balance with her loaded basket on her head, who always called out to my mother, 'Any cauld tea missus', knowing full well a hot cup would be forthcoming.

I remember a next-door neighbour who had a bedroom for their boy and girl. It contained a mattress on the floor, a bicycle frame their only toy ...

I remember getting the bird at the old Silksworth Row Cinema for reciting 'I shot an arrow into the air'. The winner was a tiny tot who sang 'Ragtime Cowboy Joe,' and put us all to shame.

Hector M. Tusnan, Lawford Road, London

* The new Workhouse in Chester Road.

Right: An advertisement for a Schoolmistress for Sunderland Workhouse from the *Sunderland Herald* of 22nd October 1858. A few weeks later The Guardians invited applications for the post of Schoolmaster in the Workhouse. His salary was to be £40 per annum compared with the £20 per annum for the Schoolmistress. The Schoolmaster also had the extra 'bonus' of 'Board, washing and Lodging in the Establishment'.

In the middle of the last century, despite receiving a grant from Parliament to help pay the salaries of Workhouse staff, Sunderland Union were criticised for refusing to pay the going rate for schoolteachers.

Life after Death

In the last century the death of a bread-winner could have dire consequences on a family. In the 1860s if a miner from Monkwearmouth Colliery was killed at work his widow would receive two shillings a week for herself and a shilling for each child for two years.

Boys at St Columba's School, Southwick in an era when many could not afford shoes.

Right and below: Both sides of a postcard for the Mayor's Fund in 1907. Mayor William Walker set up the Fund for the relief of distress in the Borough. A depression in shipbuilding had led to high unemployment. When the Fund started in November 1907 special thought was given to children in Sunderland.

From the last century the Mayor's Fund provided boots and stockings for poor children who would otherwise have gone barefoot in the winter months.

Between the wars was another period of distress. On 13th December 1927 the Fund set up a distribution centre in the old Jopling & Tuer shop in High Street East. At this time £939 5s 8d had been raised and 2,300 pairs of boots ordered. The first recipients were boys and girls from Council, Church of England and Catholic schools in Monkwearmouth, Hendon and the East End. They each received a pair of socks and boots stamped with S.E.C. (Sunderland Education Committee).

Help the Mayor to feed the Children.
By sending Subscriptions addressed to Children's Fund
Town Hall, Sunderland.

THE MAYOR.

POST CARD.

What has already been done by the Mayor's Fund since November, 1907.

Over 500,000 Dinners for needy children.

171,000 Grocery Tickets (1/- each), for Families, besides gifts in Clothing, Coals, Flour, etc., etc., during the depression in Trade.

£12,000 has been disbursed as above in twenty weeks. Owing to the acute distress, the children must still be fed. Help is urgently needed.

Mrs & Miss Ermington
34 Clyde Terrace
Spennymoor
Ferry Hill

Durham

MORAN & BROWN, SUNDERLAND.

Sunderland Ill-Clad Little Ones

A letter to the *Sunderland Echo* before the First World War reflected one local view on the deserving poor and the undeserving poor:

A friend of mine who is a teacher in an elementary school in the East End of the town tells me that for a long time he was much distressed to see so many of his boys coming to school, even in the coldest weather, in rags and barefooted. At first he tried to provide the most necessitous with boots and stockings, but this failed to improve matters, the demand increasing to such an extent that he was quite unable to cope with it. He soon realised that the parents were sending the children barefoot in order to get free boots. So he changed his tactics and asked the Inspector for the Prevention of Cruelty to Children to call upon some of the parents. The effect was magical. Boots and stockings appeared on the feet of children who had never previously been known to wear them … I should be the last to affirm that there are no cases of genuine poverty, and that family incomes are always large enough to pay for boots. I know families whose whole income goes in paying rent for barely habitable rooms and supplying a quite insufficient amount of food to its members. These are cases to which the helping hand of the charitably disposed may well be held out.

George W. Temperley
5 The Elms West, Sunderland, 3rd February 1913

Sunderland Orphan Asylum Band. The boys are dressed in sailor suits and many went on to a life at sea when they left the institution.

Single Parent

Sir F.M. Eden's Report on *The State of the Poor* in 1797 cited the case of a Sunderland man raising his family alone: 'An old man who is a shepherd on the common of this town brought up 10 children by his own labour without assistance from the parish or any one. To some of his boys he gave a decent education. His earnings were generally 5s or 6s a week, and he was chiefly employed in husbandry.'

The Report revealed what his wage could purchase in the town at this time: butcher's meat 5d to 6d per lb, new milk 1½d per quart, potatoes 10d per peck*.
* peck – a measure capacity for dry goods = 2 gallons.

Waif's Rescue Agency and Street Vendors' Club

Thousands of lads over the years have passed through the doors of Lambton Street Boys Fellowship but few might know that it was formed at the turn of the century as the Sunderland Waif's Rescue Agency and Street Vendors' Club.

Sunderland architect, Frank Caws, was entering his office in Fawcett Street one day in 1901 when he found a street urchin sheltering in his doorway. This encounter led to the setting up of a home in Lambton Street where poor children were clothed and fed. In the beginning most of those helped were newspaper sellers.

Services used to be held at the centre and one Sunday, Frank Caws was reading from the Scriptures when the sound of a fire engine was heard. One of the boys shouted 'Howay, lads, it's a fire!' Then all the boys rushed out only to return five minutes later when they discovered it was a false alarm.

The building was twice extended, until May 1931 when new premises were opened by the Marquis of Londonderry.

By 1936 the club had a membership of around 300 boys aged between 9 and 18. It was at this time the Waifs and Vendors Club became Lambton Street Fellowship.

An early scout camp at Whitburn.

A Better Life

In the summer of 1907 Colonel Vaux and his wife held a garden party at Herrington Hall to promote interest in the Boldon Home of the Church of England Waifs and Strays Society. One of the guests, Archdeacon Long, reminded the gathering of the conditions that existed in the East End of Sunderland. He thought their society was responsible for giving poor girls and boys a better start in life. 'At the present time boys and girls were prepared for emigration to Canada, where they were being sent with every prospect, of becoming useful citizens.'

An outing for disabled children organised by Sunderland Rotary Club. The club organised the first of what they called their 'Crippled Children's Outings' in June 1923, when 80 children enjoyed a day out at Rothbury and Cragside. This became an annual event and the children at the 1926 outing to Belsay Castle had a special treat when presents were dropped to them from an aeroplane.

Post-War Austerity

Times were hard on the Barbary Coast for a decade after the end of the last war. It was a common sight to see kids running about the streets barefoot. In schools like Thomas Street and Stansfield Street there were cages with racks of sand shoes. Children who could not afford sand shoes for PE (which was almost everyone) wore these. Then the next class would use the same shoes. Nearly everyone had a free school dinner even on Saturdays. We would queue up at Thomas Street with a dinner ticket and for some it was their only meal of the day. Everybody seemed to be in the same boat, making ends meet was a struggle. The 'tick' shop was a way of life for thousands. In the mid 1950s things seemed to get better. People were being rehoused on new estates and there was more money about.

Billy Dent

Marked Out

At Town End School in the mid 1960s I remember the cage which kept sand shoes in. These had yellow stripes painted across the toes. These were for those children who could not afford their own shoes for PE classes.

Tommy Johnson

Keeping Warm

Even in the 1950s and '60s some large families could not afford blankets for all the beds in the house. One of my mates said he had coats on his bed and his mam told him to say they had blankets not coats. I was in his house one day when he shouted down the stairs 'Mam, a button has come off the blanket'.

Alan Jones

Cottage Homes Nightmare

By Pat O'Brien

Whilst the older generation look back and remember the good times of their childhood I believe they don't want to remember the hard times: empty bellies, children without shoes on their feet, bad housing, no inside running water and shared outside toilets. I was born in 1943, was well dressed, had enough to eat and lived in a better part of town – Thornhill. But at 6 years of age, along with my younger sister, we were taken to Ashbrooke Towers – a children's home. A nightmare had began: stripped, hair almost all cut off and put into a disinfectant bath where we were cleaned with a scrubbing brush. Regular beatings, name calling and seemingly never-ending cruelty followed. After six months we were transferred to the Cottage Homes in the grounds of the General Hospital. Could things get worse? Of course they could.

The Cottage Homes today, when they opened on 11th June 1908 they held 150 children who would normally have been in the Workhouse. Generations of Sunderland children have been threatened with the Cottage Homes by parents when they have misbehaved. For some children the nightmare of the Cottage Homes became reality.

Force fed, beaten with hairbrushes till they snapped and made to stand outside in all weather as punishment for speaking during mealtimes. Each Cottage was run separately, Catholic Cottage was Number 4, that was us. Twice a year we went to get a new change of clothes from a building situated next to the

The Cottage Homes buildings are now used by Sunderland Royal Hospital. The five detached blocks each containing two houses were originally built at a cost of £13,000.

mortuary. All the clothes were the same, as were the shoes. We were given pocket money on a Saturday morning.

We were constantly told no one wanted us, that was why we were there. The children that were in these homes were not *bad* children. There were orphans, children whose parents had divorced and mothers unable to look after them, as well as neglected children. Even today the abuse in children's homes still continues. Will people ever listen to a child's cry for help?

After her Cottage Homes experience Pat went on to marry Gordon O'Brien and helped him build up a successful demolition business. She found time to have four children who in turn have presented her with ten grandchildren. Back row, left to right: Aaron, Danielle, husband Gordon, Erin, Alex, Michael, Nathan. Front: Kate, Sophie, Pat, Callum and Liam.

The People's History

To find out more about this unique series of local history books – and to receive a catalogue of the latest titles – send a large stamped addressed envelope to:

The People's History
Suite 1
Byron House
Seaham Grange Business Park
Seaham
County Durham
SR7 0PW